SAMBO
SYSTEMA

Russia's
Prominent
Martial Arts

An Anthology of Articles from the *Journal of Asian Martial Arts*

Compiled by Michael A. DeMarco, M.A.

Copyright © 2016 by
Via Media Publishing Company
941 Calle Mejia #822
Santa Fe, NM 87501 USA
E-mail: md@goviamedia.com

All articles in this anthology were originally
published in the *Journal of Asian Martial Arts*.
Listed according to the table of contents for this anthology:

Secours, K. (2008), Vol. 17, No. 4, pp. 30–41
Secours, K. (2004), Vol. 13, No. 4, pp. 28–51
Jacques, B., & Anderson, S. (1999), Vol. 8, No. 2, pp. 20–42
Polyakov, L., Yankauskas, I., & DeRose,D. (1996), Vol. 5, No. 3, pp. 52–59
Koepfer, S. (2008), Vol. 17, No. 3, pp. 40–49

Book and cover design by Via Media Publishing Company
Edited by Michael A. DeMarco, M.A.

Cover illustration

Artwork by Oscar Ratti
Futuro Designs & Publications ©1999

ISBN: 978-1893765290

contents

preface

R ussia is rich in martial traditions deriving from a highly diverse population. Sambo—developed by the Soviet Red Army—became the most recognize martial art associated with Russia mainly because of its presence in international competitions. Another style to become recognized for its great practicality and encompassing training regimen is Systema. Originally created for Russian Special Operations Units, Systema's teaching gradually spread world-wide after the fall of the Soviet Union in 1991. This anthology contains writings about Systema and Sambo that present essential information for anyone interested in the history, theory, and practice of these combative systems.

In the first chapter, Kevin Secours shows that ground fighting and grappling are necessary components of a complete tactical arsenal. Specific emphasis is on the role of defending the takedown in a modern survival scenario. In chapter two he summarizes the prevailing theories and findings pertaining to the science of fear as it relates to surviving violence. How these findings have been interpreted by modern combative systems in the West are compared with approaches to the traditional Russian martial arts and their application in the Russian Special Forces.

The next three chapters focus on Sambo. Jacques and Anderson detail the historical development of Sambo. Vasili Sergevich Oshchepkov, a student of Jigoro Kano, and Victor Spiridonov worked to develop this combative system. However, despite the judo-jujutsu influence, Sambo was born of native Russian and other regional grappling and combat wrestling styles bolstered with many useful and adaptable concepts and techniques from the rest of the world. This chapter presents details of the early development up to recent times.

The fourth chapter by Polyakov, Yankauskas, and DeRose focuses on some of the fundamental techniques that are legal for Sambo competition. The purpose of this study was to examine and compare the most successfully used submission techniques of three of the greatest figures in the history of sambo competition: Michael Burdikov, Alex Feodorov, and David Rudman.

Sambo has become well-known largely due to the success of Sambo fighters in various mixed martial art venues. Stephen Koepfer's final chapter offers a description of its development as well as a delineation of one of Sambo's hallmark strategies: offensive rolling. Examples of proper forward rolling and three related offensive techniques are presented.

May readers of this anthology come to appreciate the great depth of Russian martial traditions and the unique developments that emerged in the arts of Systema and Sambo.

Michael A. DeMarco, Publisher
Santa Fe, New Mexico, July 2016

— 1 —
Takedown Defenses
of Russian Systema

by Kevin R. Secours, B.A.

All photographs courtesy of
Kevin Secours, except where noted.

Introduction

The Russian martial art of Systema enjoys a unique perspective among combat arts. It enjoys heavy Asian influences from two distinct sources: both through the continuous migration of culture across its shared border with China and through the intentional efforts of the early Soviet government to research, test, and integrate Asian styles during the first half of the 20th century (Secours, 2004: 29-30). Yet, at its core, it maintains a distinctly Cossack origin, and the influence of these roots continues to influence its epistemology and combative techniques to this day, through a heavy emphasis on adaptability and unorthodox tactics. Primarily a battlefield art, Systema remains in use by the most elite units of the Russian Special Forces and increasingly continues to bear influence on law enforcement and military personnel across the globe.

In this chapter, we will focus specifically on Systema's approach to defending against takedown attempts. It is my intention to distinguish between "sport" and "combat" technique. Before addressing the particular details of the Russian method, however, I would like to contextualize the problem of takedown defense within a larger historical perspective.

The Enduring Debate

Over the past decade, there has been nothing less than an explosion of interest in the grappling arts and ground fighting, due in large part to the popularity of mixed martial arts (MMA) events. While these events have illustrated the importance of being a well-rounded fighter in all ranges of combat within the ring (Tedeschi, 2002: 10), debate continues over how fully sport technique will actually transfer to the street or battlefield.

A popular school of thought acknowledges that sport grappling is a valuable training tool for developing improved mobility; grappling maximizes the body as a delivery mechanism. The "warhead" that ultimately gets put onto the end of that delivery system, whether submission lock or street finish, can then be left to the practitioner's discretion. Others counter that the goals and limitations of sport differ too drastically from life-and-death combat to be helpful. The argument here is that overtraining ground fighting risks creating a reflex to volunteer for the ground, needlessly placing one's self in a vulnerable position. While this debate is likely familiar to most modern martial arts enthusiasts, what may be somewhat more surprising to many readers is that it is actually far from an exclusively modern concern. Stretching back well into the ancient world, the actual value of the grappling arts for combat preparation was widely debated.

The ancient Greeks were perhaps the most widely known proponents of wrestling in the ancient world. Greek culture traditionally regarded grappling as the ideal form of preparation for soldiers. Solon, the lawgiver, said that wrestlers train for the "greatest of all crowns...the felicity of mankind itself—that is to say, freedom for each person individually and for the state in general..." (Poliakoff, 1987: 96). "Freedom" here carried the most literal interpretation—freedom from invaders through military might. Wrestling, for the ancient Greeks, was the very personification of warriorhood.

This view was not universally accepted by their contemporaries, however. Plato openly stated that athletes made ineffective soldiers. He favored imitation warfare games over combat sports for soldier preparation (Poliakoff, 1987: 99). Similarly, the Spartans placed substantial restrictions on sport. As Philostratos noted, the Spartans used wrestling largely to condition the body and spirit of the young only. The Spartans knew from experience that the use of the phalanx formation in warfare meant that most soldiers suffered injuries around the extremities of their shield—largely the groin and the throat. As such, they regarded boxing as being a far more relevant form of battle preparation, in that it applied more directly to the use of the shield and taught practitioners how to parry, slip and absorb impacts (Poliakoff, 1987: 93-97). The Romans went further still in their opposition. They openly regarded wrestling and Greek sport in general as the cause of the Greek's enslavement and "degeneracy." Instead, the Romans prioritized horsemanship, weaponry use, and tactics when preparing their armies (Poliakoff, 1987: 95).

Despite these critiques, wrestling certainly did feature in the warrior training of many cultures. Moreover, in most of those cultures where wrestling was prioritized, it often involved all manner of tactics and included both standing and ground work. There is a popular conception that "stand up" grappling dominated the ancient world due to its superior battlefield application. The popular logic here is that no one would volunteer to go to the ground in the pitch of battle. Many modern advocates of this theory site the apparent dominance of stand-up grappling in ancient representations as evidence. Archaeological evidence must be interpreted carefully here, however. In the case of Greek depictions for example, most surviving examples come to us via vase paintings. The shape of these vessels and the conventions of rendering used during this period simply lent themselves more readily to depictions of stand up wrestling: "Ground wrestling scenes require solid masses of coloring, fill the space less effectively, and pose problems in perspective" (Poliakoff, 1987: 33).

Certainly, written records of the same period tell a drastically different story. Contests frequently went to the ground and no tactics were originally outlawed. Take the example of the champion Leontiskos of Messene, who won the Olympiad largely through the use of finger breaking (Poliakoff, 1987: 25). Similarly, wall paintings of wrestling scenes from the tomb of Beni Hassan in Egypt show a variety of ground fighting positions dating back to 2,000 BCE. These include a variety of leg scissors on the ground, in particular positions which modern jujutsu practitioners refer to as the "full" and "half guard." Similarly, in Japan, records of wrestling from as far back as 230 BCE clearly state that any technique was permitted in wrestling matches (Ratti & Westbrook, 1973: 230). In fact, rules pertaining to rings and outlawed tactics only appeared around 1570 (Ratti & Westbrook, 1973: 337).

Aesthetic and ideological concerns likely also play a huge role in the dominant depictions of stand-up wrestling. Standing wrestling personifies a purer representation of the sport and the ideal behind it. Even today, we see this ideal in judo where *ippon* or "full point" is granted for a clean throw where the practitioner lands cleanly on their shoulders, or in the octagon, where the average MMA fan massively prefers stand-up action over the slower and more technical ground engagements. It's easy even for a modern reader to be stirred by this simple account of Kleitomachus' victory at the Isthmian games: "In the third contest on his shoulders came no dust" (Poliakoff, 1987: 24).

This simple description resounds with us at an emotional level. It's the very personification of standing your ground that was heroically repeated throughout history, from Gilgamesh's victory over Enkidu, to Job wrestling Satan, to the most common school yard scuffle. To remain standing and in turn cast your opponent down holds a powerful place in our psyche.

When approaching the subject of takedown defense, it's important to recognize the lingering debate stretching out to us through history. Takedowns are more than just an effective or commonplace form of attack. They represent a powerful psychological statement of dominance. There is something positively primal at work here that keeps their threat ever-present. Reinforcing this instinctive sense is the familiarity for many of their high school wrestling or football experience and certainly the media reinforcement of professional wrestling and ultimate fighting. Even more relevant for us here is the reality that takedowns are also far more dangerous outside of a sporting context. Even the most basic throw or sweep carries an exponentially greater risk when performed on an unmatted surface, in an environment cluttered with furniture and other objects, as the subject's head is sent racing powerfully to the ground like a weight at the end of a whip. What can we do to counter against an opponent who tries to take us down when our lives may hang in the balance?

The Systema Approach

Since its inception, Russian Systema has included a comprehensive treatment of grappling. Although its earliest roots stretch back to the 10th century, its greatest period of development occurred following the rise of the Soviet government in 1917. During the Soviet era, the Russian government invested heavily in the research and development of their hand-to-hand combat methods. Fusing dominant elements of their unique cultural arts with aspects of Asian martial arts, they forged a highly effective hybrid geared to contemporary use (Secours, 2004: 29-30). Although accurate documentation of this period is sparse and often contradictory given the Soviet emphasis on secrecy and misinformation, we can still readily see that grappling played a central role in Russian training. The earliest versions of those Soviet era systems that were made more publically available, namely the so-called "sport" and "combat" varieties of SAMBO (*SAMozashchita Bez Oruzhiya*), which literally means "self-defense without a weapon," are based heavily on a fusion of judo and native Russian wrestling systems. Systema shares common roots with these styles but was designed to be utilized in battlefield conditions by injured or exhausted agents. For these reasons, Systema places a far greater emphasis on maximizing biomechanics and minimizing energy expenditures.

How then does this emphasis on efficiency translate into how a Systema

4

practitioner would deal with a grappler? First, emphasis in all Systema work is placed on understanding breathing and its relationship to calming the psyche and optimizing the body's reactions. As with many internal martial arts, Systema dedicates significant attention to leading the student through exercises that allow them to experiment with the role of breathing in increasingly rigorous and resistant exercises. Students learn to address the fear of falling, practicing creative ways of engaging the ground both in solo and partner work. Obstacles can be added to better replicate the dangers of the street and test psychological coping skills. Students study how to move seamlessly from standing and ground positions and how to fight effectively throughout this complete range of motion. Practice can include simply walking towards a stationary partner and falling to learn distancing and how to control relative positioning. Eventually, work evolves to dynamic and resistant partners who push and force the student to the ground. Addressing this fear is the first step to learning how to defend against takedowns.

A second psycho-physical component of takedown defense is the fear of encroachment. The moment an individual is approached by a potential opponent, the body will generally enter an automatic state of readiness. This often includes an acceleration of heart rate, shallower and more rapid breathing, and increased tension throughout the body. Systema deconstructs the various phases of this encroachment through a wide variety of basic drills involving exaggerated, slow motion approaches and evasions. Practitioners work slowly, learning to identify and respond to the earliest cues of aggressive intent in their partner. This helps educate the student's sensitivity, highlighting the window of opportunity for pre-emptive responses in the practitioner and reinforcing the ideal psycho-physical connection between effective Systema breathwork and simple, efficient movements. Students learn how to circle, pivot, and side-step, opening like a gate to bypass the takedown attempt and then "closing" behind the attacker with strikes and counter attacks.

Similarly, Systema also heavily employs the use of breathing exercises that involve wave-like contractions throughout the body. From a health perspective, these contractions allow students to increase their awareness and control and the mobility of their bodies over time, while safely strengthening their joints. Combatively, however, these same contractions can also be used to help dissipate excess tension and stress-chemicals during a crisis. Similarly, targeted contractions to select body parts during an actual grappling encounter can be used to create supports or "frames" between a defender and an attacker, to allow the space to move or escape, to better adhere and to communicate the full weight of one's body during a throw or counter, or else to bait and deceive the attacker into resisting one area of the body while moving and attacking with another.

Throughout all motions, emphasis is placed on maintaining a balanced posture and form. Many grappling arts prioritize the use of the sprawl (keeping the hips away from the opponent). Systema certainly includes these biomechanics, particularly in gun work, when diving to the ground to take cover; however, in a grappling context, Systema tends to prioritize moving away with form and posture whenever possible. This does not imply a stiffly erect stance, but rather refers to a natural preference for correct alignment. Attention is placed on simple footwork that moves in short, simple paths. The feet never cross, but stepping patterns maintain a broken rhythm and explosiveness. The body center is regarded as floating, residing between the solar plexus and the lower navel area, which allows one to maintain a more flexible center of gravity and allows for easier and more erratic directional changes, not unlike the flight pattern of a butterfly. These movement patterns are enhanced by exercises that reinforce yielding and suppleness at all times. In those instances where a student must sprawl or deviate from form in any way, priority is placed on returning to a balanced structure immediately.

Whenever possible, side-stepping and striking is favored. Systema includes a variety of unique drills that isolate and refine the mechanics of striking, paying particular attention to any chambering or contraction phases that might otherwise telegraph intent. One of Systema's areas of greatest strength is its ability to create powerful, non-telegraphic strikes from unorthodox angles, without requiring large commitments of energy from the legs or hips. Connected to this, body position is always kept balanced and mobile, without rigid stances or any loading and cocking of the physical structure.

Once contact is made, emphasis is on "close work." This includes corkscrewing strikes into the spine and areas of density along the back, neck, and head. Simple push drills against static opponents in a takedown position gradually evolve into slow movement and, finally, full speed and resistance. This progression teaches students how to locate tension in the structure of their opponent and to intercept it with their strikes for maximum effect. Quick strikes to the eyes, throat, and groin along with strong neck manipulations are prioritized. All work is designed to end encounters as quickly as possible and to always operate on the assumption that a weapon or secondary attacker may be waiting in the wings.

When sprawling or going to the ground is required, or when it is impossible to quickly break contact with the opponent, Systema practitioners strive to maintain continuous movement. Students learn how to flow with takedowns, using the energy of the action to catapult their own reversals and sweeps. Students seek to avoid locking or grabbing their opponent in any way which might otherwise limit their own mobility, in turn making them more vulnerable to secondary attackers. Unless they are required to restrain their opponent due to their profession (as with Law Enforcement Officers), they favor instead flowing back to a dominant position, quick wrenches and jamming actions, and striking with broken rhythm. In Systema, the guiding logic is that in attempting to lock your opponent, you also succeed in locking yourself.

As previously discussed, through Systema's attention to refining biomechanics, students learn how to optimize the function of each joint and to sequentially erode any tension otherwise blocking their motions. This leads to what Systema practitioners refer to as "Wave Motion"—the fluid engagement of consecutive joints in the most integrated and efficient manner possible. This work is particularly relevant at extremely close range. Against leg takedowns, this can include wavelike motions through the legs to strike with the knees and jam arms or other joints. On the ground after a takedown, it can include powerful close-range strikes with the hips, shoulders, or head. Even conventional strikes from the bottom position, which are not ordinarily regarded as effective from the bottom position, can become significantly more powerful through an understanding of this work. This can be understood in the following comparison: The majority of martial styles rely on torque and rotation from the hips to generate power. As a result, when such a fighter is pinned on his back, the limitations or inability of the hip to rotate effectively massively limits his ability to fight. At a basic level, the various chains of muscles have been trained to "fire" and trigger one another like a line of dominos, but when one part of that chain is interrupted, the remainder of the line cannot engage effectively (if at all). This is one of the main reasons boxers who have not learned to adapt their arsenal to the ground game have such difficulty throwing strikes from the bottom position on the ground. By comparison, Systema students also learn how to generate power simply by maintaining structural alignment, then relaxing the shoulder to maximize their range of motion and effectively drop the arm like a bone battering ram into the opponent. By adding even the smallest amount of muscular assistance, free of any antagonistic contraction, the actual power and accuracy delivered to the target is far greater while using far less energy.

Bruce Lee has said that so long as human beings have two arms and two legs, there will be only be one way of fighting. Fundamentally, the capacity of an arm or leg to punch or kick is limited to the essential physiology that we all share. The distinction between styles today, therefore, is not in "what" we are training, but rather in "how" we are training. At its core, Systema's approach is to not simply accept the body's fear response as its best alternative. Rather, it begins by teaching students how to eliminate tension blockages to release their full biomechanical capacity. It progresses by enhancing that physical structure with correct breathing and focus and by reinforcing the formidable power of relaxation over tension. Ultimately, from these releases comes the greatest refinement, a change in the practitioner's perception of his own potential versus all stages of the takedown. The arbitrary psychological limitations regarding grappling and the ground dissolve. Combat becomes a pure fluidity and the individual inherits a greater freedom from the many reflexive fears that previously shackled him, releasing his optimal potential.

TECHNICAL SECTION

Photographs courtesy of Vladimir Vasiliev.

Arm Jam

Systema work strives to surpass the limitations of technique and to respond to the energy of the attacker. In this instance **(1a-c)**, Master Vladimir Vasiliev greets a 2-on-1 shoot attempt by twisting his hips. In the process, he traps the inside arm and jams the elbow against his thigh **(1d)**.

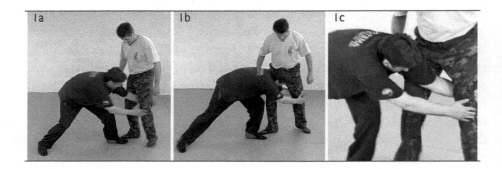

Back Fall

A key to resolving the threat of takedowns is to first eliminate your fear of falling. Here, Kevin shows a simple exercise for reinforcing correct ground absorption. Unlike many martial arts which advocate slapping the ground to dissipate impacts, Systema advocates continuous flow. Here, **(2a)** Kevin greets the ground with his hand, **(2b)** screwing the elbow into his body in one fluid motion **(2b)** then continues along the padding of his lateral muscle and **(2d)** across his shoulder to protect his spine. **(2e)** He returns to a full seated position in the same way **(2f)** unscrewing the arms in a spiral motion and maximizing all of his muscle groups and tendons, rather than pushing through linear motions that would use less of his body and encourage tension and freezing that might stop the impact in his body.

Face Punch

Here, Vladimir Vasiliev is caught with his hands low **(3a)**. Rather than chambering or cocking his hand, he emphasizes first escaping the line of the attacker's tackle and then delivering a direct, non-telegraphic punch **(3b-c)**. By keeping the body relaxed and emphasizing correct structure and breathing, Systema practitioners are able to strike non-telegraphically with tremendous power and accuracy.

Ground Flow

A key component of increasing your confidence to go to the ground is to teach the body how to dissipate force by screwing itself into the earth. In this solo exercise, **(4a)** Kevin begins in a basic low squat. **(4b)** He then collapses one knee loosely to the ground, folding onto the inner blade of the foot. This rotates the knee cap outside to protect it and uses the more reliable elasticity of the tendons and ligaments rather than depending on brute muscular strength. **(4c)** In a continuous fluid motion, Kevin slides forward from the ball of his foot onto his instep, **(4d)** then rolls over into a "hunter's squat." This simple half-kneeling position allows Systema practitioners to comfortably lower themselves without risking injuries to their hands and wrists and can be reversed to facilitate standing.

Ground Framing

Even the best shoot defense can fail. Here, Kevin has been taken to the ground. Rather than wrestle against his opponent, he creates a "frame" using his forearm to optimize the available space to move and strike **(5a)**. Then, he drives his finger and thumb into his attacker's eyes to create the space and distraction he will need to escape **(5b)**. If additional power is needed, a "compound strike" can be used, where the gouge can be placed over the eyes and then the second arm can be used to hammer the first hand deeper, like a hammer on a nail **(5c)**.

High Shoot

Here assistant instructor Danny Kovac attempts a high level shoot. **(6a)** Kevin greets his entry with a quick slap to the eyes, **(6b)** then torques his body to wrench Danny's rear arm, driving him towards the ground. **(6c)** Kevin follows-up immediately, palm striking Danny's head lower and grabbing it to facilitate **(6d)** a strong knee to the face, **(6e)** driving him back.

Neck Cranks

Neck cranks are a convenient and popular tool against shoot attempts in Russian Systema. In the first example, assistant instructor Antoine Giasson manages to get inside to clinch Kevin's legs **(7a)**. As he struggles to wrestle Kevin to the ground, Kevin slices the bone of his forearm across Antoine's eyes and nose bridge **(7b)**, locking in his second hand to maximize the crank **(7c)**.

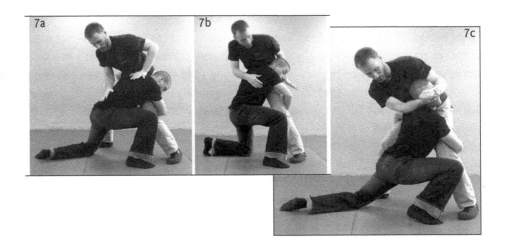

Below, Systema Grand Master Colonel Mikhail Ryabko illustrates additional neck crank variations. Here **(8a)**, Mikhail stops Kevin's shoot by driving his thumb into the nerves above the clavicle. An alternative option includes simply smearing his palm across Kevin's nose, leading him into a painful crank that stops his momentum instantly **(8b-c)**. From here, Mikhail has the option to drive a direct fist into Kevin's back, devastating his spine **(8d)**, or else he can opt to simply control him, twisting the crank to Kevin's limit until he submits **(8e)**.

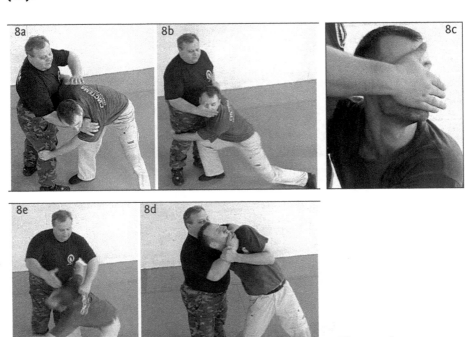

Photographs courtesy of Vladimir Vasiliev.

13

Rolling Takedown

A great exercise for gaining confidence and control of your ability to fall is to **(9a)** have your partner remain stationary in front of you. **(9b)** With slow control, lower yourself into any manner of roll, **(9c)** moving towards your partner, and **(9d)** study how you can exit your roll by trapping your partner, **(9e)** taking them to the ground. This confidence will increase your adaptability as you fall and will teach you how to go with takedown attempts and to "weaponize" your exit from the fall itself.

Rolling Over Obstacles

Another simple exercise for overcoming your fear of falling is to practice slowly moving over various obstacles. Here **(10)**, assistant instructor Michael Trussler is shown rolling over a pile of short staves.

Shoot

It is not always possible to pre-emptively evade takedown attempts. Here, **(11a)** Michael Trussler goes in low against Kevin's legs. **(11b)** Kevin greets Michael's entry, **(11c)** flowing with the takedown, **(11d)** and uses Michael's momentum against him (continued on next page).

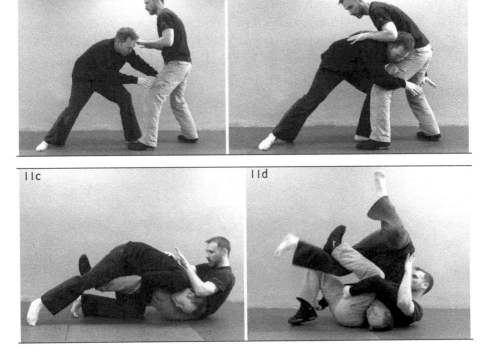

By creating a ramp with his shin, he lifts Michael over him in one continuous motion, **(11e)** landing in a dominant position, **(11f)** from where he can strike and finish the engagement.

References

Poliakoff, M. (1987). *Competition, violence, and culture: Combat sports in the ancient world.* New Haven, CT: Yale University Press.

Ratti, O. & Westbrook, A. (1973). *Secrets of the samurai: The martial arts of feudal Japan.* Tokyo: Charles E. Tuttle.

Secours, K. (2003). Russian Systema flow training: A progressive alternative to stimulus-response training. *Journal of Asian Martial Arts, 13*(4): 28-51.

Tedeschi, M. (2002). *The art of ground fighting.* Trumbull, CT: Weatherhill.

— 2 —
Russian Systema Flow Training: A Progressive Alternative to Stimulus-Response Training

by Kevin Secours, B.Ed.

... when warriors go out successfully

and come back unhurt, they

understand the art of war.

– Sun Tzu II, 1996: 124

Russian warrior.
Courtesy of K. Secours.

Introduction

In the past 25 years, more has been learned about the structure and function of the human brain than in the rest of human history combined. New insights into the process of learning, research into surviving violence, and studies regarding the psycho-physical effects of harming our own species have reshaped the way many now view combat training.

In this chapter, I will summarize the prevailing theories and findings pertaining to the science of fear as it relates to surviving violence. I will specifically compare how these findings have been interpreted by modern combative systems in the West and compare these approaches to the traditional martial arts of Russia and their application in the Russian Special Forces. It is my sincerest hope that this study will both introduce readers to a lineage of martial arts that has only recently begun to receive the exposure it deserves while enriching the readers' understanding of the neurophysiology of violence, enhancing the practice of their own chosen styles.

The Birth of the Russian Warrior Arts

The martial arts of ancient Russia were forged in the fires of adversity, across a vast and unforgiving landscape of diverse geography and climate. Finding their roots several millennia before the birth of Christ, the earliest incarnations existed as scattered practices among Slavic tribal communities. Beginning in the 6th century, a host of foreign enemies laid siege to Russia, spurring an evolution in the development of these arts. Among the most notable invaders, Bata Khan in 1237 led the Mongol occupation of Russia, which remained until the late 15th century, exposing early Slavic warriors to new military strategies and weapons (Shillingford, 2000: 21). From these encounters, the earliest Russian masters learned one simple truth: combat is a chaotic state that carries an infinite number of challenges and opportunities. The most effective way to prepare an individual to survive this adversity is through the development of adaptability, creativity, and autonomy. Since there was no way to predict how an enemy would attack, there could be no one technique or single form that could guarantee survival (Vasiliev, 1997: 14).

Reinforcing this emphasis on adaptability was the absence of a formal army to protect the people. As civilian warriors, fighters of this era required an art that was quick and easy to learn, without detracting from their daily duties as farmers, hunters, and merchants. As a result, emphasis was placed on natural movements over complex form or memorization. Russian warriors sought to be buoyant and irregular in their movement. Interestingly, the social prevalence of squatting and kneeling in the Orient cultivated a perception of the body's center as residing just below the navel. By comparison, European conditions were less demanding on stability. The potential for a higher center of gravity, alternately residing between the base of the navel and the solar plexus (what the Russian's term a "floating center of gravity") encouraged a pendulum-like use of the torso with footwork that resembled movements found in ice-skating (Vasiliev, 1997: 7, 15-17).

The goal of the Russian martial arts was always to optimize one's own biomechanics while impeding the aggressor's ability to function. Guided by this simple objective, the arts continued to evolve through the generations, passing from father to son, borrowing from neighbors and enemies alike (Vasiliev, 1997: 17).

The next greatest turning point occurred in 1917, when the newly installed Communist government forbade the practice of all traditional martial arts in the hope of further destroying the roots of nationalism in its people. Despite their outward efforts however, the government could not deny the sheer effectiveness of the indigenous combat styles. Secretly, the Communists worked to assimilate the various traditions into a single concentrated hybrid.

In 1918, Lenin founded an organization (*Vseobuch*, or *Vseobshchee Voennoye Oobuchienie* or "General Military Training") to study the various native combat traditions of the world, spearheaded most notably by K. Vorosilov, A.A. Kharlampiev, V.A. Spiridinov, and V.S. Oschepkov. To this end, teams of investigators traveled throughout the world as the government tirelessly devoted their resources to testing and refining their traditional knowledge, enhancing it to include modern tactics and weapon use. Over 25 Russian unarmed combat styles were integrated into a distilled hybrid and reserved exclusively for the most elite tiers of the Russian Special Forces (*Voiska Spetsialnogo Naznachenia*) or *Spetsnaz*. Russian combat traditions became known once again (Shillingford, 2000: 21). Its practitioners referred to this new hybrid simply as *Systema* or the System.

The Science of Survival

We are designed to survive. Evolution has hard-wired a complex personal protection system into our bodies that we carry with us everywhere we go. The reflex system's entire function depends upon our perception of a threat. While much is known about the effects of fear on the human body, little is known about the actual causes. One of the world's leading researchers on the causes of fear, Dr. Joseph LeDoux of New York University, has said that essentially fear is a "neural circuit." Fear stimuli are absorbed through our eyes, ears, and other sense organs, feeding information to the portion of the brain known as the thalamus. There, time permitting, the brain quickly creates an image of the threat in our minds, interprets this image, and then processes an appropriate response to the cortex—the portion of our brain responsible for delegating actions. This allows the most evolved "human" portion of the brain to remain engaged and rational thought to prevail. Neuroscientists commonly refer to this neurological pathway as the *high road* (Ledoux, 2004: 212-214).

A second neurological pathway also exists. In more spontaneous scenarios, if the brain regards a stimulus as being too urgent, the threat message received by the thalamus is instantly rerouted to the section of the brain called the amygdala. In these instances, the rational forebrain (cortex) is completely bypassed. Instead, the amygdala instantly responds with what is commonly referred to as the *startle/flinch* response. These are any automatic reflexes designed to protect the body from sudden harm. Startle/flinch responses include instinctively pulling your hand away from a hot stove, sneezing to clear your airway of foreign particles, or blinking to protect the eyes. Neuroscientists refer to this second protective subroutine as the *low road* (Ledoux, 2002: 212-214; Ledoux, 2004).

Initially, it may seem redundant, even ineffective to have two separate response systems in our body, but as researcher Doug Holt explains, both serve a valuable purpose. The "low road" startle/flinch response acts as a safety net that overrides cognitive control during surprise situations. This reflex sacrifices detail and accuracy for the sake of the fastest possible reaction time. In the words of Dr. Ledoux: "You're better off mistaking a stick for a snake than a snake for a stick." If instead, the brain determines that there is sufficient response time, research has shown that the signal will continue to the cortex, rational thought will remain engaged, and the forebrain can still make actions deliberately. According to Holt, the only difficulty with this "double-wiring" is that the connection from the cortex down to the amygdala is less well developed than the connection from the amygdala back to the cortex. This means that "low-road" reflexes will exert more influence on the cortex than vice versa. Once the startle/flinch response has been triggered, it is very difficult to turn it off (Holt, 2004).

How the Brain Experiences Fear

High Road Response

When confronted with a stimulus, the brain registers the information in the visual thalamus. If the brain deems there is sufficient time, the signal is allowed to pass through to the visual cortex where a decision can be consciously made, based on experience and preferences. These high road responses are slower but far more accurate.

Low Road Response

If there is not enough time to properly process the information and make a rational decision, the signal takes an immediate shortcut to the amygdala, triggering a reflexive body action. The low road responses sacrifice accuracy for a faster response time.

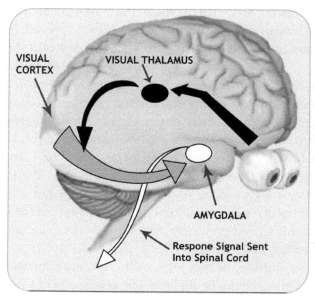

VISUAL CORTEX

VISUAL THALAMUS

AMYGDALA

Respone Signal Sent Into Spinal Cord

Understanding Combat Stress

Many of us were raised believing the myth that during extreme situations, humans will generally behave in extraordinary ways. While this may be true from a spiritual or moral perspective where adversity has been known to inspire humans to sacrifice and achieve great feats, from a purely physical perspective, the reality is that stress weakens and degrades human performance. Studies have determined that combat stress in particular triggers our basic survival mechanism, or what is termed our *fight or flight* response. Originally discovered by the Harvard physiologist Walter Cannon in 1911, this response occurs when our brain perceives a threat, whether real or imagined, signaling various glands to dump massive amounts of chemicals and hormones into our bloodstream (Cannon, 1911; Ledoux: 212-214).

As we fill with adrenaline and cortisol, our body jumps into high alert. This in turn reprioritizes body function: vision narrows to reduce distraction and intensifies to scan our environment for potential enemies. Secondary functions like sex drive and digestion are temporarily shut off. Blood flow is diverted from our extremities to reduce the risk of loss from potential injuries and channeled toward our largest muscle groups to allow us to flee or fight with more strength. Millions of nerve cells fire in a fraction of a second, arming reflexive weapons throughout our body, allowing you to run faster, hit harder, and endure more pain (Shillingford, 2000: 18).

The startle/flinch response can be triggered any time we perceive a threat, running the full gamut from the pre-fight jitters that a professional fighter might feel before stepping into the ring to the complete system override that occurs when you are drowning, when your airway automatically closes to prevent the incoming flow of water. From a combat perspective, no matter what system you train in, if your brain deems any stimulus urgent enough, your flinch response will take over. So what you are left with is:

- What can be done to direct or improve the automatic low-road responses in our flinch response? and

- What can be done to maintain rational high-road brain function, preventing the low road from being triggered in the first place?

• Punch Flinch Response

Many Stimulus Response-based training methods in the martial arts use the "Startle Flinch" response as their technical starting point. The idea at work here is that our low road responses can be linked through repetition with a trained arsenal, until the flinch response effectively becomes a trigger for technique. These approaches often rely on quick, jamming actions that oppose the attacker's force directly.

Integrating the Flinch Response in Combat Training

Military researchers in the 20th century quickly began to understand that although the effects of the startle/flinch response seem debilitating in that they reduce rational thought and fine motor skills, they ultimately serve a survival function that has succeeded in keeping our species alive for thousands of years. Western military researchers launched a move toward the simplification of combat mechanics. Gross motor movements, like large sweeping deflections and club-like hits, replaced intricate techniques. Military training in the West reinforced "universal" or "transferable" movements that could be used against a wide variety of threats with little modification. For example, a simple, windmill swing of the arm could be used to deflect a kick or punch, strike a limb, disarm weapons, or attack the body. As the soldier became more accustomed to responding under extreme conditions, the likelihood of experiencing paralysis in a life-threatening situation diminished drastically (Shillingford, 2000: 18; 41-43). The American military pioneer, Colonel Rex Applegate, in his landmark book *Kill or Get Killed* wrote: "Military experience, in combat and training centers throughout the world, has shown that the average man can be quickly turned into a dangerous, offensive fighter by concentrating on a few basic principles of combat and by advocating principally the use of blows executed by the hands, feet and other parts of the body" (Applegate, 1976: 4).

Beyond simplification, military trainers over the last century have also experimented heavily with conditioning the automatic reflexes through stimulus-response training. Simply put, this involves linking a particular stimulus or trigger with a desired response. We are all likely familiar with the classic example of Pavlov's dog, where a dog was fed every time a bell was rung. In time, the dog became conditioned to associate the ringing of a bell with food, until the bell alone was enough to cause the dog to salivate. Fire drills are another common example of stimulus-response training. Most of us have been conditioned from our early school years to line up in an orderly fashion and evacuate the premises the moment we hear a fire alarm.

Through repetition and by keeping the link between the trigger and the response clearly evident, it is possible to literally retrain our reflexes. In fact, research has shown that the repeated exposure of a subject to any stimulus, no matter how intimidating that stimulus may initially be, is ultimately capable of deconditioning a subject's anxiety response (Ornstein, 1991: 92). Simply put, familiarity eliminates fear. The military has been perfecting this form of conditioning since the beginning of the 20th century. Flight simulators, target shooting, war games using paintball guns, and first-person shooter video games are all excellent examples of modern stimulus-response training.

• Stimulus Response Training

Stimulus Response training is designed to link a successful response with a specific stimulus through repetition. A very common example of this type of training is target shooting. By using increasingly realistic targets, shooters are able to develop reflexive firing skills even under extreme conditions.

Photography by Anastasia Grouza and Najma Ali, except where noted.

One of the world's leading experts on operant conditioning* in military training is Lieutenant Colonel David Grossman (U.S. Army Ret.). A former Army Ranger and West Point psychology professor, Grossman is the author of *On Killing: The Psychological Cost of Learning To Kill in War and Society* and an active spokesperson against the effects of the media in cultivating violent behavior. Grossman notes that humans, like most species on this planet, naturally carry a built-in aversion to killing their own kind. This is a byproduct of successful evolution, since species that combine to combat their common predators are more likely to survive than those with the tendency to kill their own. Citing the research of Konrad Lorenz, Grossman notes that when animals with antlers and horns fight one another, they head butt in a harmless fashion. But when they fight any other species, they go to the side to gut and gore. Rattlesnakes will turn their fangs on anything, but they wrestle one another. Almost every species has a hardwired resistance to killing its own kind (Grossman, 1996: 6).

* **Operant conditioning:** the process of increasing or decreasing the likelihood that an individual will produce an active behavior (an operant) as a result of interacting with the environment. As defined in: Sternberg, R. (2000). *Pathways to Psychology*. 2nd Edition. Albany, NY: International Thomson Publishing.

St. Basil's Cathedral in Moscow. *Stock photograph.*

I suspect that many readers might question whether such an aversion to harming our own species exists. The sheer quantity of violence on the evening news would certainly seem to suggest otherwise. Nevertheless, the inhibition to harm has been widely recorded and researched. In his book *The Code of The Warrior*, Rick Fields cites numerous records of tribal warfare to illustrate how traditional cultures are generally reluctant to inflict harm even during conflict. He suggests that it is perhaps because of their closer connection with the cycle of life and their heightened awareness of their own mortality that they reserve the use of their own lethal capacities. While war and violent conflict historically has served a role as Fields terms a "cultural antidote" for social ills and in some cases even as an ecological balance through population control, it is quickly becoming antiquated and unnecessary (Field, 1991: 24-27). William Ury, the director of The Global Negotiation Project at Harvard Law School and acclaimed negotiations expert, echoes these findings, noting that much of the historical "evidence" of our own species' barbarism has been misinterpreted according to our own assumptions and prejudices (Ury, 2002: 11-18). We assume that our ancestors must have been more violent because they were more primitive, but the reality is that the great majority of humans have no craving to harm their own kind. Later on in this chapter, I will discuss the dangers inherent in using modern conditioning methods to undo this natural safety mechanism and show how much of the modern tendency toward harming our own is in fact due to operant conditioning methods inherent in our mass media.

The Power of Flow

> Those skilled at the unorthodox are
> as infinite as heaven and earth,
> as exhaustible as the great rivers.
> – Lao Tzu, 1998: 124

During its evolution, the Russian martial arts adopted a different approach to combat readiness. While they deeply understood from firsthand combat experience that flashy or overly complex technique simply did not work under the stress of a real fight, practitioners also believed that trying to reduce combat to two or three sure-fire predetermined moves through stimulus-response training was equally flawed in that no one response could work in every situation. Instead, the Russian martial arts sought to encourage the practitioner to discover their own natural way of moving. To achieve this, these arts relied on providing a slow training approach, where the practitioner was allowed to explore his/her body's capacities. As with stimulus-response training and most forms of learning, repeated exposure allowed the practitioner to gently erode their fears and uncertainties and replace them with familiarity.

The two main distinctions between conventional stimulus-response training and the Systema approach are that no one response is reinforced in the Russian method relative to each stimulus and that training occurs at a slower pace. Training that moves too quickly, runs the risk of only triggering the practitioner's innate "flinch" responses, reinforcing existing knee-jerk reactions and stopping the cognitive brain from functioning. This prevents new learning from occurring and permits the students to instead continually repeat their existing responses over and over again. The old adage "practice makes perfect" is simply not true. If you are practicing something badly, or performing mechanically inefficient movement, then you will only further ingrain these negative responses. Mindful, deliberate, slow practice is the only way to perfect a movement. This allows the practitioner to safely experiment with their own bodies and the bodies of their partner and to familiarize themselves with the various stimuli involved in a combat dynamic.

In Systema, fear is regarded as being more than just an abstract principle. In a very real sense, it is rather seen as a tangible energy that can be stored or released from the tissues of the body. Every training exercise, in effect, every movement in life, carries the capacity to either increase the amount of fear that we store in our bodies or else to reduce it. By learning to replace and functionalize their flinch response, the practitioner is ultimately learning to functionalize their fears (Vasiliev, 1997: 28-29). This is a view shared by many modern health practitioners who have adopted a more integrated approach to mind-body health. In *The Accelerated Learning Handbook*, Dave Meier notes that the foundation for the truly effective reeducation of our minds and bodies lies in moving away from the antiquated Newtonian worldview that regards nature as some obedient machine. He notes that the rise of quantum physics has given a new appreciation to the interconnectedness of all things (Meier, 2000: 4-5).

A host of modern physical educators have developed methods based on the holistic relationship between body form and function and the idea that the way we use our body ultimately affects its structure and health. Pioneers like Moshe Feldenkrais, Milton Tragor, and F.M. Alexander have researched how physical exercise can counter the physical effects of fear. In his ground-breaking book *Somatics: Reawakening The Mind's Control of Movement, Flexibility and Health*, Feldenkrais protégé Thomas Hanna notes that in life, our nervous system is constantly responding to various stresses and traumas in our environment with miniature muscular responses. These repeated reflexes, over time, accumulate to create habitual muscular contractions that eventually can no longer be voluntarily relaxed. These include malformation of posture, chronic stiffness, and body soreness. Eventually, the lack of use of our full potential, leads to what Hanna terms "Sensory Motor Amnesia." Simply put, we forget what our bodies are actually capable of. This in turn leads to our "gradual surrender" to the idea that we are incapable of performing certain actions and accepting that we are fundamentally limited (Hanna, 1980: xiii, 38-39).

Take the very common example of learning to fall. As children exploring our ability to move, we often fall, with little to no awareness of the harm that we may suffer. Young and supple, we are capable of surviving repeated falls throughout the learning process, but over time, the pain of falling becomes ingrained into our nervous system. We forget how to fall effectively and safely. Eventually, the stimulus of losing our balance instinctively triggers the instinctive reaction to reach desperately for the ground. In itself, this flinch response is well-intended in that it is trying to protect the body and vulnerable head from impact. However, as most martial arts that deal with ground work teach, the reflex to reach for the ground will generally injure the arms, wrists and hands during a fall. Instead, grapplers are taught how to improve the flinch response, integrating that same instinct to reach with a more fluid rolling action, through which the impact can be minimized (Tedeschi, 2002: 34). Most combat arts accept that the most constructive way to absorb the impact of a fall is to yield to your own inertia and to go with the fall, rather than trying to avoid it. Through repetition, practitioners successfully ingrain the reflex to flow rather than flinch, until they are able to fall reflexively, no matter how powerfully they are thrown (Hoare, 1980: 17-19).

• Falling I
Although our "startle-flinch" is designed to protect us from harm, it is fundamentally a fear-based response that destroys the very qualities that make us human; an upright body form and a self-conscious mind. Consider the example of a person accidentally falling. The instinctive "low road" response is to reach desperately for the ground to protect the face and head, although this often results in serious damage to the hands, wrists and arms.

Systema extends this concept of *functionalizing the flinch* to all aspects of combat. Training partners work toward their mutual improvement, offering attacks that challenge one another, without endangering themselves. A very similar concept is used in aikido, where practitioners take turns adopting roles as the defender (*uke*) and the attacker who will be thrown (*nage*) (Ueshiba, 1988). The absolute key to this approach in both aikido and Systema is to move at a pace that does not simply trigger the practitioner's startle-flinch response, but that instead keeps you just below your *reflex-trigger threshold*. This allows your rational mind (your high-road response) to remain engaged throughout your training and helps your body to explore, experiment, and discover new responses. What we term familiarity here is in effect a form of alternate conditioning for the fear circuit. Over time, slow training conditions the practitioner to perceive a stimulus like a punch, kick, or knife attack as something less threatening, helping the practitioner to remain relaxed and in an optimal performance state.

• Falling 2, 3, and 4

Most martial arts understand the importance of "functionalizing" this destructive flinch response into a more efficient and productive flow. Here we see the Systema practitioner **(1)** lowering his center of gravity to reduce the velocity of their impact, **(2)** greeting the ground with the meat of his back while protectively tucking his head and **(3)** continuing through the motion, allowing the force to carry him through the roll unharmed. Since Systema is based on the idea of yielding to force and designed for application on all manner of terrain, the rolling techniques do not involve slapping the ground with the hand or foot as is often the case in arts like judo, jujutsu or aikido.

Through slow training, Systema practitioners are better able to break combat skills down into essential sets, slowly and progressively—a process modern neurological researchers refer to as "chunking." Since the 1950s, educational researchers have known that the brain primarily learns through the use of images. Our earliest sensory experiences as children occur through the recognition of symbols that we then learn to relate to words and eventually grow into language (Piaget, 1952). More recently, it has been determined that by dividing new knowledge into skill sets, our brain is able to form clearer images for every step of a process, digesting the information more easily. In fact, research has shown that the internalization of mental images is essential to learning advanced motor skills, learning adaptability, and even to understanding the very idea of goal seeking—a concept pivotal to self-defense training and overall survival (Ewarts, 1973: 105-107).

• Yielding Photo 1, 2 and 3

A central component of Systema's training method is the idea of slow training, or training that moves at a pace slow enough to allow practitioners to explore and improve their bodies' motions. One extremely simple yet effective exercise for cultivating this awareness involves having a training partner slowly and gently push against your body. The goal here is to yield as efficiently as possible, emphasizing a balanced body form and correct breathing. Whether these pushes are generated by hand, foot, or training weapon, the objective remains the same—to remain below your "flinch threshold" so that each body part can relearn how to move.

• Stick Yielding 1, 2 and 3

A variation of the basic yielding exercise involves having your training partner slowly attack you with a stick. Since Systema finds its roots in the traditional, sword-based martial arts of ancient Russia, the art places strong emphasis on yielding and avoiding rather than blocking. In this exercise, the goal is to evade the stick as if it were a very sharp blade, avoiding all attempts to grab or stop the shaft. The stick wielders can test and improve the student through slow swings and stabs that force the partner to explore new ranges of movement and to abandon preconceived intentions in favor of spontaneous, creative responses.

While the Russian combat masters of the 10th century may not have understood the science behind slow learning, it is now obvious that their intuitive understanding of the education process was well founded. It is precisely the mindful physical exploration involved in slow training that appears to be so essential to Systema's hyper-accelerated learning curves. Modern research has shown that learning is fundamentally a frontal lobe brain activity. The frontal lobe, which is responsible for thinking and problem solving, also contains the primary motor area that control muscles throughout the body. Movement actually stimulates chemical secretions that are required to build the neural pathways necessary for learning. By more actively stimulating the frontal lobe through creative movement use rather than limiting action to a narrow set of forced repetitions, the practitioner is literally optimizing their brain at a chemical level and increasingly stimulating the learning connections in the body (Meier, 2000: 23-33).

Beyond building confidence and accelerating learning curves, slow training also helps to cultivate the reflex to yield rather than oppose force. A very simple exercise that Systema practitioners use to teach yielding involves simply standing in front of your training partner and slowly pushing against his body. The objective of this drill is to teach the body to yield in a manner that corresponds directly to the nature and degree of the force being received. Emphasis is placed on only moving what is being targeted and only to the degree required to neutralize the force. In Systema, the idea of blocking, whether in its traditional or more modernized "flinch" variation, is discouraged and regarded as an attempt to oppose force with force. Since there is always someone bigger or faster than you, the idea of blocking is ultimately flawed. Instead, Systema students learn to act like a matador fighting a bull, placing priority on escaping incoming violence.

Another basic Systema exercise used to reinforce this principle involves having a training partner slowly and deliberately attack you with a 4'-5' stick. Attacks should be kept fluid and versatile. Although it is important to exercise control and to attack without ego or malice, swings should still seek to follow through the partner's body so that he can gain a realistic understanding of the weapon's ultimate trajectory. The empty-handed partner's goal is to evade the stick as if it were a sharply bladed weapon. Emphasis should be placed on body movement and permitting the weapon to continue along its path, never opposing its force. Given the length of the stick and the versatility with which it can be used, evasion skills are put to the test and quickly improved. Initially, this drill can be performed very, very slowly. It is enough to simply practice walking out of the way of the stick, maintaining proper body alignment and balance while breathing in a slow, deep, and comfortable manner.

As practitioners gain familiarity and comfort with the drill, your partner can begin to swing more quickly and with more force. Again, it is important for the bulk of your training to maintain a pace that permits you to continue to explore and experiment with your movement rather than simply flinch and freeze. As the stick comes more quickly or at more awkward angles, you will invariably be caught off balance. In these instances, your hands or legs may naturally rise up to protect your more vulnerable head and body. What is essential here is that you do not allow this flinch response to become oppositional, since blocking a stick or blade will result in serious injury. Instead, the arms should be used to guide and gently redirect the weapons with minimal force. In this way, the limbs, along with any other surface of the body that receives an impact, can be taught to act as sensors which detect the incoming force, dictating to your body how much movement is needed to avoid harm.

The various types of Systema evasion drills are designed to aid practitioners to overcome the concern for aesthetics or specificity in their responses. A very similar idea is expressed by the 16th century monk Takuan Soho in his classic work *The Unfettered Mind*: "Although you see the sword that moves to strike you, if your mind is not detained by it and you meet the rhythm of the advancing sword; if you do not think of striking your opponent and no thought of judgment remains; if the instant you see the swinging sword your mind is not the least bit detained and you move straight in and wrench the sword away from him; the sword that was going to cut you down will become your own and contrarily, will be the sword that cuts down your opponent" (Takuan, 1986: 238). Similarly, the Systema practitioner's goal is to eliminate the various "stopping places" that can preoccupy and distract the mind and help cultivate a more fluid, instinctive and immediate response.

Another key ingredient in Systema's flow training approach is the emphasis on keeping learning enjoyable. Research has shown that learning also occurs best through play and ritualized games and not through simple rote memorization. This can be clearly seen during childhood (Meier, 2000). We enjoy the greatest intensity of learning during this period of our lives and we do it by exploring our world kinesthetically, physically interacting with our environment. As adults, we stray away from this approach, making learning more formalized and rigid. We impose the idea of memorizing on our brains, forcing it to ingrain specific actions or memorize movement or ideas, but this is not how our learning is naturally designed to work (Bruner, 1973).

• Punch Defense 1-7

By comparison, Systema seeks to maximize the practitioner's fluidity and adaptability by yielding to the incoming force.

(1) Here we see an attacker attempting to grab a Systema practitioner by the neck.

(2) As the attacker attempts to punch,

(3) the defender slips underneath the grab, delivering a whipping palm strike to the groin.

(4) As the attacker doubles over, the Systema practitioner continues the whipping motion through the body and into a spiraling downward elbow to the back.

(5) Grabbing the attacker's arm firmly with both hands, he drives a knee into the attacker's face,

(6) continuing with a wave-like stomp to the back of the knee. This compliments the pulling action on the arm,

(7) taking the attacker to the ground with a smooth corkscrewing action where he can be neutralized.

Even a casual study of animals, from tigers in the wild to your house cat, will show that they also naturally learn through play. Through mock fights with their parents and siblings and other games, animals develop and maintain their coordination and unlock their basic bodily capacities in relation to their environment—what Seitz calls their "kinesthetic intelligence." This is done safely, without injury or malice. In a very literal sense, they discover their environment through manipulation and exploration (Seitz, 1989). Similarly, Systema emphasizes that slow training should also be kept light and playful. In the *Russian System Guidebook*, Systema master Vladimir Vasiliev writes: "If you're serious when there is no threat, when a threat really does arrive you'll be left with nothing in reserve. You've used yourself up and left no more room to make the transition from civilian to warrior" (Vasiliev, 1997: 23). In this way, Systema's slow training can not only be seen as a safer and more effective way to learn, it is also ultimately a form of psychological reinforcement that bolsters the practitioner's self image and subconsciously cultivates a sense of restraint and self-control in the student.

Grappling with Flow

Another area of training where Systema's distinctions can be clearly seen is in the domain of grappling and ground fighting. Systema teaches groundwork as a set of principles and movements rather than a fixed set of techniques. Despite its Russian ancestry, we must be careful not to confuse Systema with Sambo. Given Systema's application in the Special Forces, no emphasis was placed on locks or holds, except for individuals who were training for bodyguard or security related work. Students were instead taught to reacquaint themselves with their body's capacities through unique training exercises to gradually counter the effects of what Hanna termed "muscle amnesia."

The Systema perception of fear as a tangible energy is also extremely evident in their ground fighting training. Defense from the ground carries a number of heightened stress inducers. Your attackers will generally enjoy a superior position, standing above you or pinning you. This can involve limitations to mobility, suffocation, reduced sensory capacities due to poor position, and the pain and fear associated with holds and locks. Rather than trying to teach specific counters to every possible threat, students are familiarized with the nuances of the ground. An example of a Systema exercise used to recondition a student's awareness involves having one student simply lay on the ground, then having four or five partners take hold of a limb, and begin to gently manipulate the appendages. Eventually, the movements become more aggressive pulls and twists. The intent is to improve the student and not harm him. Care is taken to avoid sudden or jerky movements, however, the goal is to aggressively stretch the recipient, taking him through his perceived pain thresholds. When performed correctly, this exercise helps students distinguish between real pain and the emotional exaggeration often associated with it (an emotional equivalent of the flinch response). The end result is massive relaxation, correction of body alignment, and a calmer and more focused mind (Vasiliev, 1997: 29).

• Kick Defense 1-6

Confronted with a standing kick attack from a seated position, **(1)** the Systema practitioner focuses on maintaining a relaxed body form and breathing to optimize his high road response. **(2)** As the attacker kicks, the defender leans back slightly, **(3)** inviting the kick to extend as he yields from its path and deflects it to his side. **(4)** As the kicker falls forward by his own force, the defender intercepts the extended leg with a whipping downward elbow strike to the kneecap and **(5)** sweeps the assailant easily to the ground. **(6)** Trapping the extended leg, he can quickly effect an ankle break to end the encounter.

Similarly, Systema practitioners experiment with being pinned and compressed in different ways to acclimatize themselves to the panic that often accompanies prone positions. By setting no limit on the attacks their partner uses, the recipients at once become conditioned to expect the unexpected, learning to respond genuinely to the situation at hand rather than trying to remember or replicate a specific technique. Rather than being driven by panic, the Systema practitioners remain calm in their awareness of their intrinsic capacities, systematically fixed on countering the body of their aggressor according to bio-mechanical principles rather than becoming preoccupied with the specifics of each attack.

Humans are fundamentally goal-oriented machines. The nature of the goals that you feed them will determine their effect. If they feed themselves failure objectives, like panic and desperation, they will become a failure mechanism. However, if they offer themselves success goals like countering one specific aspect of an attacker's leverage, improving their own position or maintaining their own breathing, they become success mechanisms. It is precisely the absence of a clear goal that leads to frustration and the rise of aggression (Maltz, 1960: 132).

• Knife Defense 1-5

Here we see how Systema's basic evasion exercises can be applied as a functional combat technique. **(1)** Confronted with a knife to the stomach, **(2)** the defender yields from the weapon's path, allowing the escape to create a deflection with the outer forearm. **(3)** Continuing the deflection along its natural path, the Systema practitioner squeeze locks the knife hand tightly against his body, digging his radial bone into the pressure points on the vulnerable inner wrist. **(4)** He continues the wave motion of the body, painfully bending the attacker's own wrist back towards him, with the full strength of his body, while delivering a stunning open-hand chop to the neck. **(5)** Grabbing the opponent's head with a downward twisting action, he then drives his body forward, maintaining the option to stab the attacker with his own weapon.

A Self-Defense Short Cut with a Cost

> That the yielding conquers the resistant and the soft conquers the hard
> is a fact known by all yet utilized by none.
>   – Waley, 1956: 238

Stimulus-response training works—irrefutably and unarguably. It has been proven to be a simple, direct, and effective approach to rapid learning. However, this neuro-physical shortcut comes with a tremendous risk. Grossman notes that through the use of operant conditioning methods, the American military was able to improve their soldiers' firing rates or their willingness to fire on the enemy from 15% in World War I to 55% in the Korean War and finally to over 90% by the Vietnam War. He cautions, however, that the cost involved in overcoming our natural inhibitions to harm include extreme rates of combat fatigue and post traumatic stress disorders. Research has even shown that just facing the stress associated with realistic combat training or with heightened states of alert, as a soldier might experience while on standby, when endured for prolonged periods of time, will likely cause psychiatric harm (Grossman, 1995). In *Achilles in Vietnam: Combat Trauma and the Undoing of Character*, Jonathon Shay similarly notes: "the specific nature of catastrophic war experiences not only cause lifelong disabling psychiatric symptoms but can ruin good character" (Shay, 1994: xiii).

The danger with stimulus-response training is that the brain's "low-road" reflex is triggered repeatedly. To react quickly, this reflex bypasses a detailed analysis of the threat—in essence, it doesn't distinguish between a real threat and a false alarm. This is why a horror movie can still frighten us—we know that the stimulus is imitated, but our brain will still reflexively respond to any sudden stimulus, like a monster jumping out on screen. Going back to LeDoux, it's better to mistake a stick for a snake, then vice-versa. The stimulus will still trigger a very real chemical reaction in our bodies. Through the same process, stimulus-response training induces all of the same chemical effects of the combat it is seeking to emulate. The more intense and realistic the simulation, the more potent the chemical dump. With every full speed flinch response that you trigger, the body is flooded with adrenalin and a host of other natural chemicals. By repeatedly subjecting your nervous system to these effects, you run the risk of inflicting actual combat fatigue and stress disorders on your body just by training (Ledoux, 2002: 295-296).

If you are a professional working in an environment where you are likely to be immediately exposed to a life-or-death situation, this type of training may be deemed a necessary occupational risk. Immediate survival skills versus the potential for long-term psychological or neurological damage may seem like a worthwhile tradeoff. If, however, your goal is the continuous improvement of your combat effectiveness combined with improved physical, emotional, and spiritual health, stimulus-response training may be counterproductive. Slow, progressive, practice provides a safer alternative for long-term training, since it minimizes the practitioner's exposure to the natural hormonal enhancers in our bodies. Russian Systema seeks a method of combat training that permits the continual improvement of the practitioner without deterioration in the normal daily functions or quality of life. As the opening page of the *Russian System Guidebook* states: "Fighting skill should evolve into an unconquerable weapon that can't be seen until used nor taken away while its practitioner is alive" (Vasiliev, 1997).

There is significant evidence that the accumulation of stress hormones in the body is ultimately harmful. Neil F. Neimark notes that over time, improperly metabolized stress hormones can lead to a plethora of nervous system disorders, ranging from headaches and high blood pressure to deficiencies in the immune system, allergies, and arthritis. He notes that, over the long run, calm awareness is ultimately far more productive than hypervigilance (Neimark, 2004). In his critically acclaimed *Full Catastrophe Living*, Dr. Jon Kabat-Zinn similarly notes that if we don't control fight or flight, it controls us (Kabat-Zinn, 1990: 254-256).

Not only is calm awareness healthier for the practitioner over the long term, it is also more natural. While the *fight-or-flight* response is a necessary reflex when confronted by a sufficient threat, it is nonetheless an exception originally intended to interrupt our otherwise optimal state and Harvard cardiologist Herbert Benson has shown that our bodies contain a more necessary instinct that counters the *fight-or-flight* response: the instinct to relax. Ingrained into our bodies from our earliest moments in the womb, we are intuitively conditioned to rest when afforded the opportunity, to conserve energy, and to recuperate. When the *fight-or-flight* reflex is not being triggered and when our body is not otherwise engaged in intense activity, it is precisely what Benson terms our "relaxation response" that is actually at work, decreasing blood flow and respiration and providing an overall sense of well being (Benson, 2000: 90-98).

Benson notes that the relaxation response is an "inducible" physiological state of quietude that can be consciously cultivated through meditation, yoga, qigong, or a host of mindful practices. Benson notes that the danger in our modern society is that our *fight-or-flight* response is constantly being triggered by the stresses in our environment, but that both responses are socially unacceptable in a conventional setting: we can neither hit our boss nor run away from him when he yells at us. The end result is a constant accumulation of the stress chemicals associated with this heightened state, without the necessary release (Benson, 2000: 97-98). While combat training does admittedly provide a greater degree of release for these stimuli than our daily workplace might, there nevertheless remains a danger in triggering this intense survival reaction without consciously training our body's natural relaxation response as a counter-measure.

Aside from serving as a vital form of self-preservation, our relaxation response also provides the martial artists interested in reflex-based training with an option: Rather than build your combat method on the startle-flinch response as many modern combative systems do for short-term gain, the choice exists to dedicate your practice to the cultivation of your body's intuitive desire to return to its natural state of alignment and harmony. Like taiji, bagua, and xingyi, Systema shows us that it is possible to approach the resolution of violence through submission and yielding rather than sheer opposition. Relaxation has been shown to actually improve the practitioner's nervous system, including reflex speed, respiration, and bio-mechanical efficiency (Lie, 1988: 116-118).

Through a commitment to relaxation and yielding and a mindful dedication to breathing and body form, progressive muscle relaxation techniques and the free exploration of combat stimuli, Systema experts in the Russian Special Forces have shown that it is possible to safely expand a warrior's combat ability and stress thresholds. The Russian military's goal was to create no less than a super soldier—a warrior capable of supreme combat effectiveness—without incurring the incremental chemical harm to the nervous system or psychological unbalancing that you would likely suffer with more conventional flinch-response training. Their success is well documented in the combat records of their Special Operations Units, who, through a dedication to Systema training methods, were able to achieve unsurpassed performance standards in some of the most intense warfare in modern history (Vasiliev, 1997).

Conclusion: Training or Trauma

> In making preparations for struggle, it is not only necessary to consider how best to prevail, but also how best to handle the aftermath of struggle, how to safeguard the fruits of victory, and how to make the best of further opportunities that arise as a result of success.
>
> – Sun Tzu II, 1998: 124

The U.S. Marine Corps combat strategy manual *FMFM1: Warfighting* states that war is: "a continuous, fluctuating fabric of activity replete with fleeting opportunities and unforeseen events. Success depends in large part on the ability to adapt to a constantly changing situation" (Schmitt, 1989: 4). Since their earliest roots, the Russian martial arts have shared this concentration on adaptability. It is in this light that they regard operant-conditioning methods as a powerful shortcut to combat effectiveness, but with an unacceptable cost. The danger inherent in reconfiguring our neural circuitry is that we are in effect depriving ourselves of true responsiveness. Rather than learning to authentically adapt to our environments, stimulus-response training risks loading us with a limited arsenal of fixed, hair-triggered responses. Moreover, as we have seen, operant conditioning overcomes our natural inhibitions against harming and killing others of our species, undoing a safeguard that millions of years of evolution have equipped us with.

Lt. Col. Grossman warns us that there is evidence of the dangers of combat operant-conditioning techniques all around us. The same techniques used by the military and many martial arts systems to overcome the inhibition to harm are similarly employed by the mass media. Grossman believes that this contributes to violence levels reaching all-time highs in American society today. While he admits that his critics are the first to point to declining murder rates, he believes that these numbers fail to take into account the advancements in medicine and technology that assist in prolonging life, distorting those figures. More telling, Grossman insists, is that aggravated assaults have increased seven fold since the 1950s. He notes that other countries are following suit. Canada's rate of aggravated assault has increased five times since 1964 and similar statistics show at least a doubling in Australia, Greece, and Europe (Tyrell, 2000).

With so much evidence of the dangers of operant-conditioning methods, we must ask ourselves, what is the ultimate goal of our training? Systema's concerns transcend simple combat mechanics. The Russian martial arts have long understood that there is an obligation to do more than simply make a warrior into a killing machine. Training must instill responsibility along with that power. It must increase humanity, not bypass it. After all, what value is there in learning to protect the self if the method you are using ultimately degrades or damages the being you are seeking to protect?

Vladimir Vasiliev, the leading Systema expert living outside of Russia, is a ten-year veteran of one of the most elite Spetsnaz teams. He served as an operative in some of his country's highest-risk missions and was an instructor for the Special Forces, KGB, and SWAT teams. Vasiliev notes that the Russian military learned the crippling cost of war from their experiences in Afghanistan and Chechnya. They sought to create a warrior that could survive the emotional stresses of combat and the key to achieving that was to promote a good moral character and a respect for human life. Systema offered one such alternative: "If you can accomplish your task without taking a life, then this is good" (Tyrrell, 2000). "With all of the aggression in the world" Vasiliev adds, "there's also a great fear of becoming a victim. The Russian system tries to free the student of this fear and protect him from the even greater terror of becoming an aggressor" (Vasiliev, 1997: 14).

Systema achieves this through its comprehensive "slow-training" approach, eroding the fears of its practitioners by respecting our natural inhibition against harming our fellow man. By "functionalizing the flinch" response dissolving their fear, practitioners are able to achieve a state of intuitive flow and surpass the boundaries of ego and self-consciousness, where truly optimal performance is unleashed (Csikszentmihalyi, 1990: 106). From the authentic responsiveness of the flow state comes the capacity to care and assess, to sense and decide, and ultimately to experience the world around. In the end, the goal of the Systema practitioner is to protect the self, not to harm another.

Bibliography

Applegate, R. (1976). *Kill or get killed*. CO: Paladin Press.

Benson, H. (2000). *The relaxation response*. NY: Harper Collins Publishers.

Bruner, J. (1973). Organization of early skilled action. *Child Development*, 44, 1-11.

Cannon, W. (1911). Mechanical factors of digestions. *American Journal of Physiology*, 27: 64-70.

Csikszentmihalyi, M. (1990). *Flow and the psychology of optimal experience*. NY: Harper and Row.

DeBecker, G. (1997). *The gift of fear*. NY: Dell Publishing.

Ewarts, E. (1973). Brain mechanisms in movement. *Scientific American*, 229, 103-110.

Fields, R. (1991). *The code of the warrior*. NY: Harper Perennial.

French, S. (2003). *The code of the warrior*. MD: Rowman and Littlefield.

Gardner, H. (1983). *Frames of mind: The theory of multiple intelligences*. NY: Basic Books.

Grossman, D. (1995). *On killing, the psychological cost of learning to kill in war and society*. NY: Little Brown.

Grossman, D. (1999). *Stop teaching our kids to kill*. NY: Crown Publishers.

Hanna, T. (1980). *Somatics: reawakening the mind's control of movement, flexibility and health*. CO: Perseus Books.

Hoare, S. 1980). *Judo*. NY: Random House.

Kabat-Zinn, J. (1990). *Full catastrophe living*. NY: Bantam Doubleday Dell Publishing Group.

Ledoux, J. (2002). *Synaptic self*. NY: Penguin Books.

Lie, Foen Tjoeng. (1988). *Tai chi chuan, the Chinese way*. NY: Sterling.

Lorenz, K. (1963). *On aggression*. NY: Harcourt Brace and Company.

Maltz, M. (1960). *Psychocybernetics*. NY: Simon and Schuster.

Meier, D. (2000). *The accelerated learning handbook*. NY: McGraw-Hill.

Ornstein, R. (1991). *The evolution of consciousness*. NY: Prentice Hall Press.

Piaget, J. (1952). *The origins of intelligence in children* (2nd ed., M. Cook, Trans.) NY: International Universities Press.

Seitz, J. (1989). The development of bodily-kinesthetic intelligence in children: Implications for education and artistry. Paper presented at the American Psychological Association Convention, New Orleans, LA.

Schmitt, J. (1989). *FMFM 1: Warfighting*. DC: Department of the Navy, United States Marine Corps.

Shay, J. (1994). *Achilles in vietnam: Combat trauma and the undoing of Character*.

NY: Simon & Schuster.

Shillingford, R. (2000). *The elite forces handbook of unarmed combat*. NY: Thomas Dunne Books.

Soho, Takuan (1986). *The unfettered mind*. NY: Kodansha America.

Sun Tzu. (1998). *The illustrated art of war*. (T. Cleary, Trans.), MA: Shambhala.

Sun Tzu II. (1996). *The lost art of war*. (T. Cleary, Trans.), NY: Harper Collins.

Tedeschi, M. (2002). *The art of ground fighting*. CT: Weatherhill Publishing.

Ueshiba, K. (1988). *The spirit of aikido*. (Unno, T. Trans.) Tokyo: Kodansha International.

Ury, W. (Ed.), (2002). *Must we fight: From the battlefield to the schoolyard—a new perspective on violent conflict and its prevention*. CA: Jossey-Bass.

Vasiliev, V. (1997). *The Russian system guidebook*. Visalia, CA: Optimum Training Services.

Waley, A. (1956). *The way and its power: a study of the Tao Te Ching and its place in Chinese thought*. London: George Allen and Unwin.

On-Line Sources

Holt, D. (2004 April 2). The role of the amygdala in fear and panic. Downloaded from http://www.serendip.brynmawr.edu/bb/neuro/neuro 98/202s98-paper2/Holt2.html.

Jacques, B. (Nov./Dec. 1999). My special assignment (Originally published in *Grappling Arts International Magazine*). Downloaded on April 15, 2004 from www.russianmartialart.com.

Ledoux, J. (2004 April 15). Memory and emotion. Downloaded from http://www.cns.nyu.edu/corefaculty/LeDoux.ph.

Neimark, N. (2004 April 10). The body/soul connection: Health and healing for the mind, body and spirit. Downloaded from http://www.mind-bodymed.com.

Tyrrell, M. (November 2000). Violence researcher ask communities to fight media violence at the grass roots level. *York Daily Record*. Downloaded May 15, 2004, from http://www.killology.com/army_psychologist.ht.

Vasiliev, V. (2004 March 10). About the System. Downloaded from http://www.russianmartialart.com.

ACKNOWLEDGMENT

A special note of thanks goes to Anastasia Grouza and Najma Ali for their photographic services, and to those who assisted in the technical section photographs: Franco Russo, Derek Lloyd, Jordan Bill, Jean Francois Campeau, Dan Bingham, Jimmy Koliakodakis and, above all, to Vladimir Vasiliev.

— 3 —
The Development of Sambo in Europe and America

by Brett Jacques, Ph.D. & Scott Anderson, B.A.

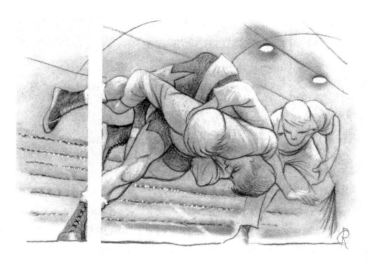

Illustrations courtesy of Oscar Ratti.
© 1999 Futuro Designs & Publications

. . . everyone saw the similarities between sambo and judo, but no-one was prepared for the effect that the Soviets were going to have on the evolution of judo over the next twenty-five years. To say that they were unorthodox is an understatement. and it was particularly their numerous variations on arm locks which took everyone by surprise. Up until this time a flying *juji-gatame* (cross-shaped arm lock) had never been seen in competition, but it was apparent that they were very well-rehearsed moves from a very highly-trained team.

– Adams. 1989: 9

Sambo: sport wrestling, permitting the application of painful holds: also a means of self-defense in a fight against a stronger or armed enemy. (Composed of an abbreviated form of the word SAM [*ozashchita*] and the initial letters of the words B[*ez*] and O[*ruzhiya*].)
– *The Dictionary of the Russian Language*, Institute of Russian Language. USSR Academy of Sciences. Vol. IV

Sambo practitioners wince when a well-meaning martial arts savant describes sambo as Russian judo, or better yet, Russian combat judo. That is akin to describing karate as Western boxing with kicks. There is a relationship, of course, but more like third cousins thrice removed.

Sambo's founders deliberately sifted through many of the world's martial arts to augment their military's hand-to-hand combat system. One of these men, Vasili Sergevich Oshchepkov, taught *judo* (the "gentle way") and karate to elite Red Army forces at the Central Red Army House. He had earned his *nidan* (second-degree black belt) from judo's founder, Kano Jigoro, and used some of Ueshiba Morihei's philosophy in formulating the new Russian art.

Kano Jigoro derived judo from jujutsu to be both a sport and a system of physical and moral education that could preserve the Japanese martial tradition and be readily used for self-defense. Kano had observed that jujutsu had been in decline since at least the 1871 Decree Abolishing the Wearing of Swords. Kano started jujutsu practice when he entered Tokyo Imperial University and encountered some of the larger hooligans in the area. Jujutsu would strengthen his body while giving him the techniques needed to beat larger adversaries. Unfortunately, the dojo of the day were often haphazard in their teaching, and it was not uncommon for senior students to brutalize the initiates as part of their own training.

> In my youth I studied jujutsu under many eminent masters . . . each man presented his art as a collection of techniques. None perceived the guiding principles behind jujutsu. When I encountered differences in the teaching of techniques, I often found myself at a loss to know which was correct. This led me to look for an underlying principle in jujutsu, one that applied when one hit the opponent as well as when one threw him .... I discerned an all-pervasive principle: to make the most efficient use of mental and physical energy.... I again reviewed all the methods of attack and defense I had learned, retaining only those that were in accordance with the principle .... The resulting body of technique, which I named *judo* to distinguish it from its predecessor, is what is taught at the Kodokan.
>
> – Kano, 1989: 16

In 1882, Kano opened the Kodokan to teach his judo. He was twenty-two years old and used space in the Eisho Temple on eight straw mats (*tatami*). In his first year, he had nine students. He did not call his art jujutsu because he hoped to break away from the stigma of the past. His new system was simplified and logical. By 1885, he had perfected his concept of *kuzushi* (unbalancing the opponent prior to initiating a technique) that would allow his students to beat almost any practitioner of the remaining jujutsu schools. Whereas jujutsu concentrated on winning, judo would concentrate on physical and moral development through kata (prearranged technique sequences) and *randori* (competitive free-sparring). The self-defense techniques were collected into the *atemi waza* (striking techniques) and taught after students mastered the art's basic precepts.

Although Oshchepkov was a student of Kano Jigoro, he never considered judo to be the perfect art that could not be improved. The Russo-Japanese War ended in 1905 when he was thirteen years old, and his home on Sakhalin Island became a Japanese trophy of war. Oshchepkov was orphaned and was educated in a seminary where he had time to learn judo from the local master. In that dojo, Oshchepkov's fighting skills caught the eye of the visiting Kano who permitted him to enter the Kodokan in 1911. Oshchepkov's arrival was not welcomed by many of the other Kodokan students. He was forced to earn his *shodan* (first-degree black belt) as much with his blood as with his sweat. This trained him to look for weaknesses in the art and his fellow students that he could exploit to survive on the tatami. He won his fellow students' grudging respect, eventually earning his nidan. In 1914, he entered the Russian military as an English and Japanese interpreter. He immediately started judo clubs and implemented the innovations and improvements that would aid sambo in its evolution.

However, despite the judo/jujutsu influence, sambo was born of native Russian and other regional grappling and combat wrestling styles bolstered with many useful and adaptable concepts and techniques from the rest of the world. As the unfortunate buffer between Europe and Asia, Russia had more than ample opportunities to sift through the martial skills of various warrior cultures. Earlier Russians had witnessed the martial prowess of the Vikings in the west and the Tatars and Genghis Khan's Golden Horde from Mongolia in the east. The regional, native combat systems included in sambo's genesis are Tuvin *kuresh*, Yakuts *khapsagay*, Chuvash *akatuy*, Georgian *chidaoba*, Azerbaijanian *gulesh*, Moldavian *trinte*, Azeri *kokh*, and Uzbek *kurash*, to name a few. The foreign influences included Dutch Self-Defense (a European version of Javanese Pentjak Silat), various styles of Catch-as-Catch-Can wrestling, savate, muay thai, wushu, jujutsu, and other martial arts of the day, plus the classical Olympic sports of boxing and Greco-Roman and free-style wrestling. Sambo even derived lunging and parrying techniques from fencing.

Fencing was included because sambo's founders recognized that swordsmanship and unarmed combat have been linked throughout the ages. The samurai of feudal Japan needed their jujutsu for the occasions when they did not wish to harm an opponent or when they were unfortunately swordless on the battlefield. Fencing concepts, such as the lunge, had already been incorporated into savate to increase its striking distances.

Sambo's early development stemmed from the independent efforts of Oshchepkov and Victor Spiridonov to integrate the techniques of judo into native wrestling styles. Both men hoped that the Soviet wrestling styles could be improved by an infusion of the techniques distilled from jujutsu by Kano into his new style of jacket wrestling.

In 1918, Vladimir Lenin created *Vseobuch* (*vceobshchee voennoye obucheni* or "General Military Training") under the leadership of N.I. Podovoyskiy to train the Red Army. The task of developing and organizing Russian military hand-to-hand combat training fell to Moscow Military District Commander K. Voroshilov. Voroshilov had been a key organizer of the Cheka in 1917. In 1923, he implemented the *OGPU/NKVD* (successors to the *Cheka*) physical training center, Dinamo.* Spiridonov was a combat veteran and officer in World War I, and one of the first wrestling and self-defense instructors hired for Dinamo. His background included Greco-Roman (then called Finnish-French) wrestling, American Catch-as-Catch-Can wrestling, Pankration, European-taught jujutsu, and many Slavic wrestling styles. As a "combatives investigator" for Dinamo, he traveled to Mongolia, China, and India to observe their native fighting styles.

* Note: These organizations are predecessors of the KGB secret service.

In 1923, Oshchepkov and Spiridinov collaborated with a team of other experts on a Soviet Government grant to improve the Red Army's hand-to-hand combat system. Spiridonov had envisioned integrating many of the world's fighting systems into one comprehensive style that could adapt to any threat. Oshchepkov had observed Kano's distillation of Tenjin Shinyo-ryu and Kito-ryu jujutsu into judo when the art was a mere twenty-five years old, and he developed the insight required to evaluate and integrate combative techniques into a new system. Their development team was supplemented by Anatoly Kharlampiev and Ivan Vasilievich Vasiliev, who also traveled the globe to study fighting arts. Ten years in the making, their catalogue of techniques was instrumental in formulating the early framework of the art that would eventually be called sambo. Here, Oshchepkov and Spiridonov's improvements on Russian wrestling slipped into the military's hand-to-hand-combat system and, later, to a greater degree, the development of sport sambo.

Sambo's birthdate is listed officially as November 16, 1938, when the All-Union Committee of Physical Culture and Sport recognized sport sambo (at that time, the sport was still called freestyle wrestling). A. M. Rubanchik was the first president of the All-Union sambo section. Sambo training was conducted by units in Moscow, Leningrad, Kharkov, Saratov, and Baku.

Kharlampiev is often called the father of sambo. This may be largely semantic since only he had the longevity and political connections to remain with the art from its inception as "*sam*," to "*samoz*," to "*samba*," and finally "*sambo*." Actually, it was Spiridonov who first referred to the new system as one of the "S" variations cited above. He eventually developed a softer, more "aikido-like" system called *samoz* that could be used by smaller, weaker practitioners or even wounded soldiers. Spiridonov's inspiration to develop samoz stemmed from an injury that greatly restricted his ability to practice sambo or wrestling. Refined versions of samoz are still used today or fused with specific sambo applications to meet the needs of Russian commandos.

Each sambo technique was carefully dissected and evaluated for its merits. If found acceptable in unarmed combat, the technique was refined to reach sambo's ultimate goal to stop an armed or unarmed adversary in the least time possible. Thus, the best techniques of jujutsu and its softer cousin, judo, entered the sambo repertoire. When the techniques were perfected, they were woven into sambo applications for personal self-defense, police work, crowd control, border guards, secret police, dignitary protection, psychiatric hospital staffs, military, and commandos.

These applications were often further subdivided. Sambo devoted time to developing teamwork in police and internal security applications. It was crucial that officers and agents not work against each other when arresting dangerous fugitives or spies. Sambo designed and rehearsed rescue tactics for comrades being attacked by armed or unarmed assailants. It was important that the rescuer act quickly without worsening the situation. Here again, teamwork enhanced tactics. If the victim was also trained in the rescue tactics, he could aid his rescuer(s) in his escape.

Many applications had specific situational or occupational techniques. For example there is a series of techniques to be used by bureaucrats and other officials who might be attacked while working at their desks. Particular emphasis was paid to using the environment (i.e., using the desk, the chair or a pen) as both weapon and shield.

Ironically, the military applications developed defensive techniques against weapons that quickly became offensive techniques with the same weapons when they were stripped away from their attackers. A partial inventory of this weapon training includes bayonet fencing; clubs; knives; shoulder bags; handguns; and unconventional weapons, such as entrenching tools; hats; belts; jackets, and chairs.

Sambo was a combat system that developed a sport version to condition the troops and allow them to practice combat techniques in a relatively safe environment. In Russian, sport sambo is "*bor'ba sambo*" and is often translated as sambo wrestling. Although the military used the term sambo in the 1930's,

Oshchepkov originally called the sport "free wrestling" or "freestyle wrestling" (not to be confused with the Olympic sport of today) and did not officially adopt the name sambo until 1946. In that same year, Kharlampiev assumed the presidency of the All-Union Sambo section.

In this transition period, combat sambo and wrestling sambo did much to assimilate each other's techniques. However, neither application absorbed the other entirely. The combat system adapted to field conditions while the "freestyle wrestling" specialized in the limited warfare engaged in on the competitive mat.

> The Great October Socialist Revolution opened the way for the further development of national forms of wrestling. By the 1930s, study of the national and ethnic forms of wrestling had already led to the recognition of the need to create a new, all-union form of wrestling which might assist in resolving the task of preparing Soviet youth for work and for defense, and at the same time might give to wrestlers of various ethnic groups and nationalities the possibility of meeting in the sports arena.
> – Chumakov, 1988: 22

These were dangerous times for the Soviet Union, and the government wanted a civilian populace that had "sport" skills that could be readily translated into military skills for perceived external threats from Nazi Germany or even Finland. The Soviets were always paranoid about all their neighbors, including the Baltic States and Romania. This presented the opportunity for civilians to practice the new Russian fighting system. Individual championships were first held in 1939, and team and individual championships in 1949. The first team championships featured fighters from eight Soviet republics plus Leningrad and Moscow. The Dinamo team won.

Two world wars and relative geographic isolation permitted sambo to develop uninfluenced by later judo philosophy and technique revisions. Also, in the late 1930's, the Soviet Union took on a siege mentality and recoiled defensively against foreigners and outside influences. The Soviet Government wanted all things great to have a Russian or Soviet origin-including their martial arts. There was no room in sambo for techniques attributed to Japanese masters. With his judo nidan and contacts in Japan's Kodokan, Vasili Oshchepkov did not survive the purges of 1937.

Kharlampiev became Oshchepkov's successor in developing the sport, and he began to scour the obvious oriental and European references from the sport system. The old name of freestyle wrestling was replaced with a new politically safer name, sport sambo, with its obvious true Russian connotations.

Eventually, samboists deemed their sport sufficiently perfected to test it on the international scene. The only international style of jacket wrestling was sport judo. In 1957, the Soviets won competitions against their East Bloc satellites Hungary and East Germany. When sambo fighters emerged from their Soviet isolation onto the mats of the 1962 Essen European Judo Championships, the Old World immediately noticed the similarities between the two fighting systems. However, the judoka saw so many differences that samboists were at best considered unorthodox. Nonetheless, the Soviet team took third place in the event, capturing five medals. A. Kiknadze of Tbilisi won the title of Absolute Champion of Europe.

Considered too unorthodox to be a part of judo, sambo's international stature was uncertain until 1968 when FILA (the International Amateur Wrestling Federation) adopted the sport as the third international style of wrestling alongside freestyle and Greco-Roman wrestling. This was hindered by the scant amount of sambo knowledge and experience in the Western world. Until very recently, combat sambo was cloaked in secrecy under the mantle of Soviet national security. This sometimes included sport sambo and slowed its exportation from of the Soviet Union.

> It was the arrival of the Russians ... which changed many of the traditional attitudes, at least outside Japan. Here were fighters who had very different training methods, and who were accustomed to picking up opponents at any opportunity. They were not worried whether the techniques had proper Japanese name (sic) or not. Their aim was to throw their opponents flat on there (sic) backs and *ura-nage* [shoulder-throw] was just as good as *seoi-nage* as far as they were concerned. Furthermore, they trained for this, both physically and technically.
>
> This fresh view prized open competition judo. Suddenly, nothing seemed sacred any more. Top champions suddenly became concerned about coming in with a strong forward attack for fear of being unceremoniously dumped backwards.
>
> – Van de Walle, 1996: 17

Judo vs. Sambo

Judo techniques **(A)** and sambo techniques **(B)** can be very similar.

A   B

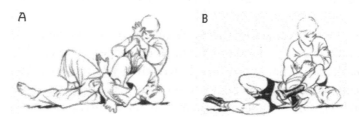

Sambo technique as Ura-Nage Variant

From the traditional tie-up **(CI)**, the attacker initiates the wrestler's duck-under **(C2)** to the side crotch-lift position **(C3)**. He raises his opponent off the ground **(C4)** to bring him down into a submission position **(C5 & C6)**.

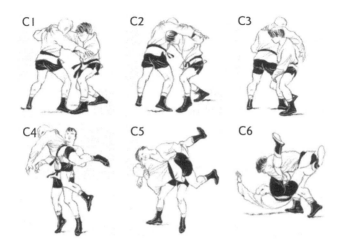

> However, it was only recently, during the 1960s, that the Russians revolutionized modern-day judo with their unorthodox techniques derived from sambo wrestling, thus opening up a whole new range of ideas for modern judoka.
>
> – Adams, 1989: 8

"Pickups" in judo refers to the group of techniques including *morote-gari*, *sukui-nage*, *ura-nage*, *kata-garuma*, etc. that are considered wrestling techniques as opposed to techniques true to the spirit of judo. However, properly executed, a pickup does score the same point as a classical judo throw.

Through Oshchepkov, the Soviets were well aware of traditional judo training practices, but did not always find them practical for their purposes. Sambo training was based on traditional wrestling instruction bolstered with the latest Western athletic training science and philosophy. The wrestling model was particularly useful to the Soviets since much of their military was already versed in their own ethnic styles of wrestling. The curriculum was based on learning to use and counter the techniques most likely to be encountered on the streets or battlefield. It started simply and progressed in range and depth of techniques based on the individual student's training needs.

Under the influence of people like Kano, the Japanese perfected the concept of the "martial art," where perfection of technique could lead to personal development and enlightenment. The Russians perfected the concept of combat survival. They did not train to perfect the technique, they trained to become proficient with the technique in all situations. The Russians understood that a partner who is compliant in kata could be quite perverse as an actual adversary. Multiple attackers would somehow not be in the designated places at the right time as specified in a kata.

Kano's genius in creating judo from the many jujutsu styles was in simplifying the techniques and scouring away redundant and overly complex techniques. Kano was always tinkering with the right mix of kata and randori to train his students. He and Oshchepkov were both proponents of kata as a means of training students. However, most of Oshchepkov's fellow combatives investigators were satisfied with simply drilling the techniques. They deemed the practical, fluid, and unchoreographed applications found in competition a superior training vehicle to hone the reflexes and instincts that fighters needed to survive. In that, they were more like the old jujutsu instructors who concentrated on winning above all.

The Soviets developed a combative calculus to handle all the variations that could occur in real life. They relied on kata only in the most general sense. When they studied the shoulder throw, they explored all the variations at one time, so the student would not be confused or thrown off by minor deviations in execution. It was not important to perfect the shoulder throw; it was important to knock the adversary down and control, damage, or kill him. Instead of hard and fast rules, they developed rules of thumb to guide the fighter. Because real life is not the controlled classroom, their motto became "philosophy, not plan."

Samboists supplemented their techniques and tactics with psychological conditioning, aerobic conditioning and weight-resistance training. In sport, it might be enough to be a technical fighter, but in actual combat it was better to be a tough, technical fighter.

The Russians explored techniques from all angles with but one prejudice: a technique must be effective and able to be integrated smoothly into a fighter's overall repertoire. Standing techniques were examined to see if they could be executed as groundwork and vice versa. If a technique, such as a sweep, were executed with a foot, could a variation be developed using a knee or a hand? In which situations might that version apply?

The traditional taxonomies of other martial arts were checked for relevancy in modern times and conditions. The primary condition of acceptance remained: could a technique down the adversary quickly and totally?

If the big lifts of Olympic wrestling filled the role, then so be it. These techniques may appear initially to be dramatic demonstrations of physical power, but like most judo techniques they are often ingenious combinations of setups, grips, footwork, and timing. Thus, the high double-leg take-down and the snatch double-leg take-down became variants of morote-gari, while the suplex became an ura-nage variant.

> . . . favored by Soviet fighters, probably as a result of their tradition in Sambo wrestling. It [a grappling-style approach to judo] involves getting the most possible amount of body contact, closing right in on an opponent and putting him under severe pressure to make a mistake. Aesthetically, it is certainly not as appealing as the traditional style, but there is no denying its effectiveness.
>
> – Seisenbacher & Kerr. 1997: 92

Russian Flying Arm-bar
From a traditional tie-up, the sambo player begins a strong leap upward, leading with his right leg **(D1)** to bring his left leg up and over his opponent's head **(D2)**. He maintains his grip on his opponent's right arm with both of his hands. Torque and gravity begin to unbalance his opponent to pull him down **(D3 & D4)** into the cross-body arm lock **(D5 & D6)**.

Judo rules and strategy centered on securing the throw. To a much greater extent, sambo fighters worked for the submission. The Soviets often used the throw or take-down specifically to set up the submission. The sambo equivalent of judo's throwing *ippon* ("one point") is called "ultimate victory." One full point immediately ends a judo bout when one fighter scores ippon or when the cumulative value of one point is earned in a match. Where the ippon may be scored with a sacrifice technique, such as tomoe-nage, a samboist must remain standing to score an ultimate victory with a take-down or throw.

Judo submissions often came from *jime-waza* (chokes and strangles). In sport jujutsu and judo, chokes are different from strangles. The former cuts off the flow of blood to the brain, while strangles cut off the air supply to the brain.

A good technique may be both a choke and a strangle. An excellent technique may be a choke, a strangle, and a joint lock all at the same time. Judo banned leg and ankle locks from the sport although they were common in striking techniques. Sport sambo banned chokes and strangles, while combat sambo used them extensively, but not to the degree found in the oriental arts. Aleksandr Kadocknikov noted this difference:

> Popular judo choke holds using the collar of the clothing are based upon the national peculiarities of the kimono costume with its wide, loose-fitting lapels. For this reason, under our conditions, with buttoned-up collars, thick lapels, and frozen fingers, it's not worth the trouble to misuse exotic holds....
> – Kadocknikov, 1992: 4

Kadocknikov was referring to another native Russian system that he taught under the All-Union Federation of Russian Martial Arts (FBRA) at the RETAL Center for Russian Martial Arts in Moscow. RETAL also had programs for judo, sambo, and Kadocknikov's system combined with sambo for specific military applications. His comments are relevant because this system is a Spiridonovian samoz derivative that influenced the striking, blocking, and kicking aspects of sambo. Many of sambo's kick counters may appear to be generic grappling but are made unique by the system of blocks and evasions.

Judo vs. Sambo

Many judo techniques use the gi extensively to help execute a throw or to choke (Note **[E]** tori's body position is raised to demonstrate the use of hands on uke's lapels), while many sambo players' combat chokes do not require the use of clothing at all **(F &G)**.

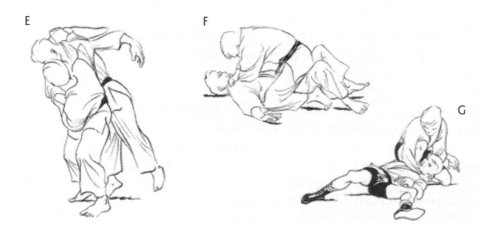

E   F

G

54

In judo, ippon may also be scored from an *osae-komi waza* (a hold down) technique; but in sambo, the hold down may only score points. Depending on the duration of the hold down, two or four points may be scored in the match one time by each opponent. A twelve-point lead scores ultimate victory. Only if the hold down causes a twelve-point lead can the hold down end a match. This reflects sambo's combat philosophy. Hold downs seldom end actual conflicts in the real world. That an adversary is trapped on his or her back does not alter the fact that the samboist applying the technique is only free to leave if the person on bottom is willing to let him go.

In combat or on the streets, if the fighter on the bottom can hold on to his adversary on top until his comrades arrive to help, then the person on top has lost the encounter. In sambo, a proficient fighter easily moves from a hold-down position to a submission hold to end a contest. That is the preferred method of winning in the sport as well as the real world.

The common ground for submissions in both arts are *kansetsu-waza* (arm locks). Since sport sambo never allowed chokes or strangles, this part of the art became adept at snagging arm locks from all angles and positions. Many judoka were surprised, and thus dismayed, by sambo's single-minded quest for the arm lock-including the flying arm bars of *juji-gatame* (cross-body arm lock). Worse, the Russians did not even use the traditional *kumikata* (grips) used on the judo mat. The sambo fighters grabbed and threw their opponents by their belts or trousers (Adams, 1992: 11, 15,56). The Soviets did wrestling picks and double leg take-downs to score ippon, or minor points to set up their submissions. This was very disconcerting to the European judo world.

> Sambo has no strangles, but what it did allow were armlocks, and the Russians wreaked absolute havoc with their clinically efficient juji-gatames, sometimes brought off from the standing position! Their judo was characterized by its unorthodox flavor, but they had many fighters with good, strong *koshi-waza* (hip techniques), frequently performed by taking an initial grip on the opponent's belt, and had considerable success in the early years with their specialized version of ura-nage, which they imported from sambo.
>
> – Seisenbacher & Kerr, 1997: 167

Clothes may make the man, but the uniform defines the sport. Both Kano and Oshchepkov designed their practice uniforms to be hardier, standardized versions of their native dress. The *judogi* was patterned on the traditional kimono, and the tighter fitting *kurtka* (jacket) was intended to represent both modern Western dress and the military tunics common in that era. The gi's looser fit is ideally suited to sport judo in both setting up the classical throws (*harai-ogoshi*, *osoto-gari*, etc.) and *jime-waza*. As sport judo evolved judoka consequently became more adept at using the gi against their opponents. Rules evolved to allow more opportunities for the classical throws to be made. Eventually, much of this throwing technology wormed its way into the art's self-defense portion whether it was street practical or not.

The kurtka was designed along the lines of uniforms that soldiers might encounter in combat, or that secret agents might find on guards, civilians or soldiers. Military uniforms are designed for function and not to give an adversary an opportunity to grapple in a clinch.

However, for sport matches, all samboists wear the prescribed uniform: boots (*sambofki*), kurtka, and shorts. This allowed for fair play and enabled the referees to judge the severity and risk of injury from sambo's potentially crippling leg locks and Achilles tendon stretches. The color of the uniform (matching kurtka, belt, and shorts) for each player is designated in advance of the match, so that one fighter wears a red uniform and the other blue. This enables both the judges and the audience to better observe the scoring techniques of the fighters. The tighter fitting kurtka complements the scrappier, lower-to-the-ground fighting style found in sambo, but inhibits the secure grips needed to perform the classical judo throws and chokes.

For example, morote-seoi nage did not truly come into its own until Kano introduced the judogi. Many judo schools had been using tighter fitting short-sleeved jackets that were popular in old jujutsu dojo. These jackets made lapel grabs difficult while having no sleeve grip at the wrist. In classical jujutsu, this throw was of little value because these gripping points were generally not available on an armored opponent. It took the judogi and sport judo to bring the throw into the limelight (Nakanishi, 1993: 10).

In US national sambo matches, the uniform color is strictly enforced. Many international competitions permit white kurtkas to be worn providing that the prescribed belt color is used. Some competitions allow the use of white shorts to release the fighters from having to leave the area to change.

European judo adopted a two-color uniform system to add contrast for matches to been seen on black and white television (Seisenbacher & Kerr, 1997: 168). The uniform colors giving the best contrast were blue and the traditional white. In 1988, this two-color system entered the realm of international competition at the European Judo Union Championships in Pamplona, Spain. Other western judo organizations have been using the two-color system on a trial basis. The traditional judoka of Japan have not been pleased by the introduction of this European innovation, but sport judo's worldwide popularity has diluted their influence in the last half of this century. Sambo competitions were first broadcast in the era of color telecasts, and the red and blue contrast was adopted.

When the Russians fought on the judo mat, they wore judogi, but cut much closer to the body like the kurtka. Their early successes led many Europeans to adopt similarly tailored jackets, and the unorthodox pickup attacks became more prevalent. In 1990, the International Judo Federation amended its existing rules to enforce the requirements for the traditional larger judo jacket (Adams, 1992, Appendix: 7,95).

Another factor may be the size of the judogi. If you look at the size of the jackets on the participants in the Tokyo Olympics and compare them to the jackets on the participants in the Seoul Olympics, you will see that the closely fitting jackets of Seoul made gripping very difficult. Often it would be possible to get a grip to make an attack, but if the attack was not successful, the opponent was able to break the grip to defend against further danger until he had resumed his balance. The changes in the rules governing size of jackets in 1990, may result in a comeback for combinations in top competition (Yamashita, 1992: 47).

Kano's judo introduced a grading system that used colored *obi* (belts) to indicate a practitioner's level of proficiency. The many belt colors of today evolved slowly. In 1886, Kano's most senior students wore a black obi to distinguish themselves from the other students, but these obi were the sashes worn with the traditional kimono. Kano did not introduce the standardized judogi until 1907. With it came the modem martial arts belt; however, it came in only two colors: white and black. Other colors (green, brown, etc.) were introduced as judo was exported to other nations.

Kano wanted the color levels to act as positive feedback for the students' progress in judo testing. Instructors would be able to assess training requirements for students based on the standardized techniques required for the award of each obi. This innovation spread to other Japanese martial arts, but was only introduced into sport sambo in 1979 by HAS (International Amateur Sambo Federation) in a bid to enlist more judoka in sambo competitions. These sambo belts were ceremonial and used to indicate a fighter's achievements in national and international tournaments. FIAS dropped the competition belt system in 1987, but many American sambo organizations, such as the American Association of Martial Arts and the American Sambo Academy, have instituted belt systems to track their members' training.

The old Soviet system recognized eleven degrees of "black" belt. A national champion was awarded a black belt (sixth-degree) onto which was sewn symbols representing the host country and organization for the event. A PanAmerican champion or other continental champion was also awarded a black belt, but at the seventh-degree level. A gold medallist in the World Games earned a gold belt (tenth-degree), a silver medallist was awarded a silver belt (ninth-degree), and a bronze medallist earned a bronze belt (eighth-degree). The eleventh-degree belt was gold like the tenth-degree belt but adorned with honorary ensigns.

Judo's philosophy, and therefore its desired arsenal of techniques, is enhanced by its deliberately engineered rules and uniforms. Judo and sambo are analogous to Greco-Roman and freestyle wrestling. Judo and Greco-Roman wrestling appear more elegant to outside observers because their rules are designed to encourage the high-amplitude techniques that please crowds. Sambo techniques include all of the major judo techniques, as freestyle wrestling contains all of the Greco-Roman wrestling techniques.

Incidentally, sambo contains all of the Greco-Roman and freestyle wrestling techniques. A chart, called the "Wheel," catalogues all of the arts that fed into sambo's development with all of their techniques. When new sambo applications are needed and techniques from existing applications are lacking, samboists go back to the Wheel to research the needed techniques to design a new sambo application.

High-amplitude throws do not comprise a large percentage of the actual scoring techniques used in sambo or freestyle wrestling because of the lower stances required to guard against pickup attacks. This difference makes high-amplitude attacks far riskier and therefore rarer.

The jujutsuka of feudal Japan would not be fazed by sambo's take-downs. Many of the techniques were commonplace then and there. However, the distillation of the art that led to judo was too refined to entertain these techniques as good martial arts. Other samurai skills did not enter judo's curriculum either. The *hojojutsu* (tying arts) and *taihojutsu* (police arts) presently practiced by the Tokyo police and their elite tactical units are such arts. Many of these skills are retained today in combat sambo.

American sambo organizations began in the 1970's as sport sambo clubs that realized that the overall art contained a vast variety of techniques outside of the sport realm. These organizations often had members who had received sambo training in the Soviet Union as part of cultural exchange programs. Also, many members were wrestlers interested in adapting their grappling skills to self-defense. American sambo was born as a new application of the Russian martial art. It is usually heavily influenced by sport sambo supplemented with techniques from wrestling, judo, jujutsu, taekwondo, and US military hand-to-hand combat systems already familiar in the United States.

Sambo is often the archive for techniques that have been lost in other arts. Many of the catch-as-catch-can wrestling styles once prevalent in North America included submission techniques such as neck cranks, toe holds, and bent arm and leg locks. Eventually these techniques were deemed dangerous, made illegal, and have long since dropped from the modern wrestler's repertoire. Many of these techniques exist in sambo.

Most of the joint manipulation and locking techniques streamlined into judo and aikido have sambo equivalents. However, these equivalents are often performed in a style closer to that of jujutsu from the first quarter of this century. This is neither good nor bad, but it is different from the modern Japanese interpretation of the techniques.

In Japan, sambo could be ignored—almost. Since the 1960's, judo has softened its position on barring judoka from forcing players to the mat simply to grapple. Sambo was probably the first wake-up call followed more recently by reality-based fighting events such as the Ultimate Fighting Challenge (UFC), where judoka have not fared as well as they might have. Oddly enough, sport samboists have fared remarkably well in Russian reality-based fighting events but have not translated that success to the international scene.

A point worth noting: American amateur wrestlers, with their strong tradition in catch-as-catch-can wrestling, have enjoyed great success in reality-based fighting events leaving both judoka and samboists far behind. Some of the wrestlers have been trained in American sambo. For example, Dan Severn is a black belt under the American Association of Martial Arts. Often criticized for their lack of finishing techniques, the wrestlers dominate their matches with their take-down skills and control their opponents until they can be finished with boxing skills or rear naked chokes. Since the only "finishing" techniques found in modern amateur wrestling are pins and falls, it should not be surprising that the wrestlers do not have traditional submission skills taught at the lower levels of other martial arts.

Sambo, judo, and even wrestling do not tolerate mat work that does not actively lead to hold downs or submissions. Unlike the UFC, the bouts are limited to no more than six minutes each, so that fighters must work aggressively to earn points to decide the outcome of a match if there is not a submission, pin or throw to a fall. Unlike the UFC, if the mat judge decides that the groundwork is stalemated, the match is halted and restarted with both fighters in a neutral position. Both fighters are then in a situation where they must work to score or be penalized. This is kinder to the audience at least.

In consonance with world level Greco-Roman and freestyle wrestling matches, international judo bouts are five minutes in length without breaks or periods. The power judo players of Europe are lobbying for four minute matches, but this is being countered by traditional judoka who prefer besting an opponent with excellent technique instead of simply overpowering him (or her). International sambo matches are six minutes in length without breaks or periods. The extra minute was deemed necessary to offset the additional difficulties of beating an opponent by ultimate victory with twelve points vice ippon by one point.

In the United States, judoka ignored sambo thanks to their relative isolation from the Russians. Also, the United States sided with the Japanese lest the Kodokan frown on its fledgling judo programs. Many of the early Americans who participated in international sambo competition came from the ranks of AAU wrestling. This stemmed largely from the AAU declaring sambo the fourth style of wrestling in the United States. Besides freestyle and Greco-Roman, the United States practices National Collegiate Athletic Association (NCAA) Catch-as-Catch-Can wrestling, which is native to North America and is often referred to as "folk style."

The wrestlers' domination of American sport sambo is changing. When the US Judo Association (USJA) implemented its policy to award belt promotions for martial arts outside of judo, sambo was quickly adopted under its umbrella. USJA Sambo belts were first awarded in 1995. Unlike the USJA's well documented judo and jujutsu programs, USJA Sambo does not have a set curriculum. It does not specify if it covers sport, self-defense, or both. Further, it does not specify if it is Russian Sambo, American Sambo, or both. Today, judo and wrestling clubs from all over the United States participate in most regional and national AAU Sambo events.

In Europe, however, sambo was always a force to be reckoned with even if sambo had been declared a wrestling style. In Russia, wrestling, judo, and sambo were considered to be the same thing: grappling (freestyle wrestling again). Just because you changed the uniform and limited some of the rules, you did not stop the athlete from doing what he or she did best. The Europeans countered the Soviet invasion of judo by modifying their sport philosophy to take in sambo's more effective techniques and methods.

Their tradition in sambo (which is similar to judo although it has a different look and feel) gave the Russians a head start over most of Europe and it still stands them in good stead today.

– Adams, 1992: 15

The distinguishing characteristic of western judo is that it does not aspire to the perfect form embodied in the Gokyo, but rather adapts it and modifies it to be more effective at throwing the opponent. The Japanese... argue that their goal is not, in fact, the same, since the aesthetic element is of intrinsic importance to the performance of any technique and if the use of force is excessive, rather than truly rational, then the object has not been achieved in accordance with the basic philosophical tenets of judo.

– Seisenbacher & Kerr, 1997: 50

Even so, it is not necessarily a smooth transition from sambo to judo, or judo to sambo.

In comparing sambo with judo, I found that on the whole judo techniques were on a higher level. But, I also discovered that the ura nage and juji gatame used in sambo were considerably more powerful and effective than those in judo. Another thing that I noted was that because the stance in sambo is wide, the samboist is vulnerable to forward-and-back combination techniques particularly to those like *tai otoshi, ko-ouchi-gari*, and *o-uchi-gari*. Thus, I was able to take advantage of the weak points of Russian judoists when I met them in contests.

– Sato, 1986: 243

Sambo's relative disregard for the hold-down did not always prepare a samboist to develop the skills needed to evade a judoka's skillful osae-komi waza. The judo hold-down is just as effective as the arm-lock in ending a bout. In turn, judoka experienced problems coping with sambo's rules and unique techniques:

I was competing in the All-Japan Sambo Competition. I was fighting the Soviet Champion and I must have tried something like kouchi-gari into yoko-tomoe-nage combination, but it came out like this [*furikotomoe-nage*] instead. I threw the Russian twice for what in judo terms would have been ippon, but in sambo terms was only four points for each throw-one point short of outright victory. In the event, my opponent caught hold of my leg and I lost on a leg-lock.

– Kashiwazaki. 1992: 43

To clarify: four points or one good throw was required to win in this manner. One point (*ippon*) ends a judo match. A twelve-point lead in the score immediately wins the sambo match. Three four-point throws often end many European sambo matches. Either way, a third throw of the type cited by Kashiwazaki above would have won him the bout if he had not submitted to the leg-lock.

Only about a quarter of the Japanese submissions in judo come from *kansetsu-waza*. This is as true today as it was in 1920 and 1960. European judo maintained this ratio until the sambo infusion of the 1960's. Since then, it has allowed kansetsu-waza to take over almost sixty percent of judo submissions. In sambo, roughly sixty percent of the submissions come from arm locks with the other forty percent resulting from pinching the hamstring or Achilles tendons or locking the knee or hip (Polyakov, Yankauskas, & DeRose, 1996; Adams, 1989: 6).

Many sambo techniques and methods of generating speed and power are better suited to the European physique than judo. Kano's martial art is based upon economies of motion, leverage, and energy to generate the most force to throw the opponent with the least amount of energy. However, the footwork and body positions favor bodies that have long torsos but short arms and legs, as the average Japanese has. Europeans and North Americans often have long or short torsos with long arms and legs.

> Because of physiological differences, it is difficult for the European to make use of concentration [of force] in a strike as is customary in the East. Therefore. this requires greater physical force. The low Eastern stance is uncomfortable for the European, with his long legs: on the other hand, for his long arms, penetrating lateral strikes are preferable. And it is on these characteristics that the Russian style system is partially constructed.　　　　　　　　　　　　　　– Kadocknikov, 1992: 52

From the Japanese point of view, note this explanation of the Japanese proficiency at seoi-nage:

> ...the strain is taken by a combination of good posture, strong thighs, and a light balance. These qualities are promoted by the characteristic Japanese body type: short arms and short legs. The legs, always seen as playing a major role in seoi-nage, are developed by a lifetime of getting up from sitting on the floor—very different from a life spent getting out of chairs. This cultural difference still determines the difference between the Japanese seoi-nage and the way it is practised in the West.
> 　　　　　　　　　　　　　　– Nakanishi, 1993: 9

Westerners who do not have a build that corresponds to that of the average Japanese are often forced into bad judo form, which is inefficient, and thus loses power and speed. Sambo adapted its techniques to take full advantage of the longer legs and arms of the average European. These included techniques that use the hands to sweep an opponent's legs out from under him. Many of these techniques derive from Mongolian or Chinese wrestling styles that used jackets but were little influenced by Kano's innovations or philosophy. An advantage shared by both the Chinese and Mongolian styles is that their techniques are not dependent on the opponent's gi or other garb to be effective.

Also, by including the full arsenal of wrestling techniques, the samboist opens up a wider range of attack techniques and follow-ups. For example, if a samboist cannot complete an ouchi-gari style attack because his opponent steps over the technique, the samboist may follow up with a "knee pick" to the swept leg. In turn, he may pull that trapped knee over his hip, catch his opponent's far arm, and switch to a harai-ogoshi equivalent throw against the opponent's standing leg. Done properly, the throw should lead directly to an ankle or leg lock off the pick or throw.

Additionally, as Westerners entered judo, their different builds caused them to attempt classical judo throws, but forced them to adapt their styles and techniques to be successful. Traditional judoka did not always meet these adaptations with open arms and smiling faces. Consider the case of uchimata:

> During the 1950s, uchimata proved the highest scoring technique at competitions in the Kodokan. This was partly caused by the absence of weight categories and the discovery by taller men that the leg form of uchimata could be especially effective against smaller opponents... and to highlight uchimata as a tall man's throw, which did not do full justice to its potential range of application. Long legs also promoted the use of ken-ken uchimata, though this variation was often disparaged as a second-class technique and referred to as *shomben uchimata*, or the "urinating dog style"—not the kind of variation that appealed to purists and lovers of fine judo. Yet then, as now, no-one could deny its effectiveness.
> – Sugai. 1991: 14

This last variation of uchimata is a standard workhorse of both sport and combat sambo. Whereas ken-ken uchimata is considered flawed for judo because the technique lacks amplitude and altitude for the *uke* (receiver of the throw), it is a philosophically correct technique for sambo. The Russian art prefers a lower amplitude throw where amplitude is traded for decreased time for technique execution. This quickly positions the opponent for a submission in the event that the throw is not scored as ultimate victory. In self-defense situations, the lower amplitude techniques take less time to execute and allow the defender to more quickly deal with multiple attackers—or to more quickly overcome a single attacker.

Like sambo, European judo began to adapt to its environment:

> A major difference between judo in the East and West is the sprung floor that is common in all Japanese dojos . . . The effect of the sprung floor is to encourage movement and spring to allow the judoka to train with less fear of injury, and to move faster, and without inhibition . . . The typical western judo club mat is slower . . . and, because taking falls is harder, players tend to be more defensive and attempt to pin their opponents in place, rather than moving with them.
>
> – Seisenbacher & Kerr, 1997: 75

Oshchepkov did not import tatami to Russia to use in his training areas. Instead, he used the wrestling mats already familiar in the West. The differences between the mat and the tatami caused a sambo bias toward wrestling-style attacks instead of judo-style throws. Also, the wrestling mats facilitated the matwork and submission orientation that set sambo apart and ahead of judo in those aspects.

Sambo did not appear on the world scene under its own banner until the first international tournament was held in 1967 at Riga, Latvia, in the then Union of Soviet Socialist Republics (USSR). However, this event only featured teams from the Union of Soviet Socialist Republics, Mongolia, Yugoslavia, and Bulgaria. The second international tournament was held in 1969 and featured competitors from the United Kingdom and the Netherlands as well. The Japanese fielded their first sambo team at the fourth international tournament in Tashkent, Uzbekistan, in 1971.

Judo held its first world championships in 1956. In 1964, it became an official Olympic sport spurring worldwide interest in the art and in improving its techniques for competition. Interest in striking techniques (*atemi waza*) waned as judoka devoted greater training time to improving their competitive techniques that were now gaining more and more importance in belt promotion requirements.

The first sambo world games were held in Tehran, Iran, in 1973. Sambo made its brief Olympic appearance as an exhibition sport in the 1980 Moscow games. By the middle of that decade, it was evident that sambo would not join judo as a permanent Olympic sport. The samboists who had basked in the limelight of 1980 had no other choice but to take up judo if they dreamed of winning other Olympic gold medals with their hard-earned skills. They did so enthusiastically, changing both sports.

In more recent times, there has been an increase in the techniques of sport judo, largely as a result of the influence of Russian fighters coming into the sport with their traditions of sambo wrestling. This eclectic quality has always been Judo's greatest strength. When confronted by anything new and of value, it has always been capable of assimilating it.

– Seisenbacher & Kerr, 1997: 30

In reverse osmosis, sambo's best techniques were absorbed into European judo and via European judo into Japanese and ultimately, American judo. Now, belt throws, single-leg picks, double-leg picks and crotch lifts are common in European judo championships, and Europeans acknowledge the sambo origins of their new found techniques. The line between sambo and judo in Europe is blurry at best, and at worst, unseen.

Following the emergence of the Russians as a force to be reckoned with in international judo, the trend has been towards a gradual sharing of success among European countries, with an increasing number of the world's nations sharing out the honors in international tournaments, generally at the expense of the Japanese.

– Seisenbacher & Kerr, 1997: 168

Originally, European judoka were dismayed to have East German and other Soviet Bloc athletes block their ogoshi and uchimata with the sambo wrestler's rear-crotch lift. Not only did the judoka adopt this technique for both a counter and an attack, but they also learned to adapt ogoshi and uchimata to the Russian inside/out throw to block the rear crotch lift.

The inside/out throw, as a hip throw, is performed by blocking the attacker's right elbow with a right hand—so that the thrower can step in front of the attacker but be behind his right arm—and wrap his left arm around the attacker's waist. The throw may be executed as *ogoshi* (large hip throw), *hane-goshi* (hip spring) or *uchimata* (inner thigh reap). If altitude is not the object, stepping across the attacker's left shin with the left leg, while shoving down and leftward against his trapped leg, will also force the attacker to the ground. The thrower may even use the *tai-otoshi* (body drop) throw from this grip. The chief advantage of this cross-arm throw is that the attacker is severely limited in counter-techniques while being set up for very quick and brutally efficient arm, leg, and ankle locks. This same throw, without the leg assists, had long been employed in Greco-Roman wrestling, but had not been included in the original judo by Kano Jigoro. However, variants can be found in jujutsu and aikijutsu.

Russian Inside/Out Throw

From an outside slide block **(HI)**, the thrower steps across and under his opponent's right arm **(H2a; H2b** as viewed from opposite side) to lift his opponent for the throw **(H3 & H4)** where he lands in a submission position **(H5)**.

Today, the two sports are in no mortal danger of merging, but they have not finished their cross pollination. In 1997, martial arts audiences were treated to two bold experiments aimed at improving and vitalizing their respective arts: New Sport Judo and American Modified Sambo. Both of these revised sports preserve their roots while incorporating rules and elements from other martial arts—including each other. They were designed to entertain audiences, attract newcomers, and provide fun but more realistic arenas for the fighters themselves. In the US, sport sambo is undergoing further name changes. In 1998 AAU/US Sambo Association (USSA) events, American Modified Sambo was renamed Combat Sambo. In 1999, it will be called Modified Combat Sambo.

Sport judo and sambo are different arts that share some common ground in take-downs, throws, arm locks, and Europe. Many great judoka, such as Sato Nobuyuki, Kashiwazaki Katsuhiko, Neil Adams, and Peter Seisenbacher, have integrated sambo techniques into their championship repertoires. Today, most of sambo's world champions have relied on judo techniques to score points and to win matches and championships. This is especially true in Europe, where almost every samboist also plays judo.

The future of jacket wrestling will continue to evolve as the styles and techniques of the two arts blend and adapt. Ironically, this is happening now with New Sport Judo and American Modified Sambo in the greatest of all melting pots: the United States of America.

References

Adams, N. (1989). *Judo masterclass techniques: Armlocks.* Wiltshire, England: Crowood Press.

Adams, N. (1992). *Judo masterclass techniques: Grips.* London: Ippon Books, Ltd.

Batts, O. (1997). Combat sambo, Russian martial art. Cambridge, England: Pendragon Press.

Chumakov, E. (1988). *One hundred sambo wrestling lessons.* Moscow: Physical Culture and Sports Publications.

Craig, D. M. (1995). *Japan's ultimate martial art: Jujutsu before 1882—The classical Japanese art of self-defense.* Rutland, Vermont: Charles E. Tuttle Company, Inc.

Inokuma, I. and Sato, N. (1986). *Best judo.* New Yark: Kodansha International.

Kadocknikov, A. (1992). *The Russian style of martial art.* Kiev, Ukraine: PR1.

Kano, J. (1989). *Kodokan judo.* New York: Kodansha International.

Kashiwazaki, K. (1992). *Judo masterclass techniques: Tomoe-nage.* London: Ippon Books, Ltd.

Liederman, E. (1923). *The science of wrestling and the art of jiu jitsu.* New York: Earle Liederman.

Lukachev, M. (1998). Creation of sambo (born in Tsar's prison to die in Stalin's one). *Physical Culture and Sport,* 9-10, 91. Downloaded from website http://cclib.nsu.ru/projects/satbi~e/statyi/sambo.html.

Nakanishi, H. (1993). *Judo masterclass techniques: Seoi-nage.* London: Ippon Books, Ltd.

Polyakov, L., Yankauskas, I., and DeRose, D. (1996). The variety of submissionholds developed and applied by leading sambo practitioners. *Journal of Asian Martial Arts,* 5(3), 52-59.

Seisenbacher, P. and Kerr, G. (1997). *Modern judo, techniques in east and west.* Wiltshire, England: Crowood Press.

Sugai, H. (1991). *Judo masterclass techniques: Uchimata.* London: Ippon Books, Ltd.

Van de Walle, R. (1996). *Judo masterclass techniques: Pick-ups.* London: Ippon Books, Ltd.

Vasiliev, V. (1997). *Russian system: Inside secrets of Soviet special forces training.* Visalia, CA: Optimum Training Systems.

Yamashita, Y. (1992). *Judo masterclass techniques: Osoto-gari.* London: Ippon Books, Ltd.

— 4 —
The Variety of Submission-holds Developed & Applied by Leading Sambo Practitioners

by Leonid Polyakov, M.A.,
Ionas Yankauskas, Ph.D., & Dayn DeRose, M.A.

Sambo (also *sombo*), an acronym for the Russian phrase *"sambo oborona bez oruschia"* (self-defense without weapons), was made an official sport of the Soviet Union in 1939. This article focuses on some of the fundamental techniques that are legal for sambo competition. The willingness of sambo players and coaches to experiment with hitherto little known Slavic, Central Asian, and Mongolian wrestling techniques produced an unusual repertoire of techniques that were to explode on the international judo scene in the sixties. The first Soviet international judo competitors were samboists wearing judogi and adapting to judo rules. Their unorthodox style and technique caused shocking wins over Western Europe's champions, and an amazingly strong performance by Soviet judo (sambo) players in the 1964 Olympics.

The success of sambo's participants in the research and development of new techniques, rather than only relying on tradition, is grounded in observation, cataloging, and comparison of successfully applied techniques. The purpose of our study is to examine and compare the most successfully used submission techniques of three of the greatest figures in the history of sambo competition: Michael Burdikov, Alex Feodorov, and David Rudman.

Scoring Methods
Sambo is the only major wrestling style in which a win by "pin" does not exist. Matches resulting in total victory can be won outright by:

1) a throw of the opponent cleanly onto the back and shoulders. The opponent must bodily leave the mat before landing and the thrower must remain on both feet.

2) a joint lock or painful hold applied to the opponent's arms or legs, which causes the opponent to surrender. Choking is illegal. Because of the possibility of overly stubborn samboists allowing themselves to be hurt rather than surrender, any great involuntary noise made because of inflicted pain is considered a submission.

The Three Samboist Chosen for Study

Ironically, Burdikov, Feodorov, and Rudman are the heros of a society that, during the Soviet years, did its best to keep their achievements quiet. The uncomfortable truth is that, because sambo is both a sport and a method of military training, many aspects of sambo were classified inappropriately (by Western standards) as military secrets. This may sound mysterious and exciting, but its function was to irritate and frustrate publication; research; and those wrestlers, judoka, and samboists who merely wanted to educate themselves. All three of the gentlemen mentioned in this treatise attained the title of "Honorable Master of Sport" and "Honorable Coach." These titles indicate that not only have they won in international competition (all three are former world and European champions), but they have reliably produced international champions while acting as coaches.

To give some perspective as to the three nearly equivalent standings in sambo, Honorable Coach Rudman, perhaps the foremost of the three, is regarded by Russian samboists in the same light as the Japanese Kimura Mashiko or American Dan Gable. In the former Soviet Union, he is at least as well known as Alexander Medved, the four times Olympic Gold Medalist who stunned the wrestling world by throwing 400-pound American Chris Taylor (over twice his weight) by a suplex (essentially a dropping neckbridge) and simultaneously setting the Olympic record for fastest pin. Rudman's peers are elite company, indeed.

Sambo was originated in the former Soviet Union and is one of the most popular sports there. It is also increasing in popularity as a sport in the United States. In its land of origin, sambo is considered one of the most exciting and physically demanding sports. Though its origin is a synthetic combination of freestyle wrestling, Greco-Roman wrestling, judo, and other martial arts, it has developed many of its own unique techniques.

To find the most efficient way to perform submission holds and to implement them into training of sambo wrestlers, the results of the three most distinguished samboists were compared at the 1984 sports training camp in Vilnius and at other numerous tournament locations and dates. A total of 156 holds were cataloged and broken down into 13 categories. The greater percentage of the submission holds observed were those applied to the upper body (arms) (59%, see Table 1). The rest were applied to the lower body (legs) (40.4%, see

SAMBO RATINGS

Third level	=	beginner
Second level	=	local champion
First level	=	regional champion
Master of Sport Candidate	=	national level player
Master of Sport	=	national champion
Honorable Master of Sport	=	international champion

Table 2). The data shows that, out of the second group of submission holds, 71.4% of the submissions were locking techniques for the knee and pinching of the Achilles tendon and cuff muscle. Eighteen different techniques, or 28.6%, can be grouped into five categories: hip locks, outside leg knots, foot locks, hip muscle pinches, and hamstring stretches. The following figures demonstrate the number of holds out of the total number (156) of submission holds performed: Feodorov: 52=39.7%; Rudman: 61=39.1%; Burdikov: 33=21.2%.

David Rudman introduced 38 variations of submission holds for the arms. When the variety of holds are compared, Rudman preferred elbow locks (42.1%) as opposed to the five other kinds of possible basic locks: arm knots (7.9%), reverse knots (2.6%), shoulder locks (23.7%), and bicep pinches (23.7%). Feodorov demonstrated 35 technical variations of submission holds for three categories of upper body submission holds: elbow locks (54.3%), arm knots (5.7%), and shoulder locks (40%). Burdikov demonstrated 20 variations of submission holds of four kinds for the arms: elbow locks (55%), arm knots (20%), shoulder locks (20%), and bicep pinches (5%).

The data in Tables 1 and 2 shows the following tendencies: Rudman's successful application of submission holds concentrated more on arm holds (40.9%) than Feodorov (37.6%) and Burdikov (21.5%). Of the combined number of submission holds on the arms, Feodorov demonstrated more techniques for shoulder locks (20.4%) than Rudman (16.2%) and Burdikov (11.8%). More categories of submission holds on the arms were observed for Rudman (41.7%) than for Burdikov (33.3%) and Feodorov (25%).

The analysis of the correlation between kinds of submission holds on the legs used by Rudman, Feodorov, and Burdikov show that Rudman demonstrated 23 kinds of submission holds on the legs, using six different variations. Mr. Rudman relied more heavily on sophisticated variations of the Achilles tendon pinch, cuff muscle hold (30.4% each), knee lock (13%), hip lock (17.4%), and outside leg knot (4.4%). Feodorov demonstrated 27 variations of execution for submission holds on the legs using six types: knee locks (37.1%), Achilles tendon pinches (22.2%), hip locks (11.1%), cuff muscle pinches (7.4%), outside leg knots (14.8%), and hamstring stretches (7.4%). Burdikov demonstrated 12 variations of execution for submission holds on the legs using six kinds, but greatly relying on only two: cuff muscle pinches (38.5%) and knee locks (23.7%). The remaining groups of submission holds (hip locks, Achilles tendon pinches, outside leg knots, and hip muscle pinches) accounted for the remaining percentage (38.4%).

Feodorov made more use of advanced technical variations of submission holds on the legs (42.9%) than Rudman (36.5%) and Burdikov (20.6%). All three of these distinguished sambo wrestlers used submission holds on the legs in exactly the same amounts of variations (33.33%).

Technical Section

New Principles for the Application of Submission Holds as Applied by Selected Leading Samboists

The pedagogical observation shows that three submission holds were being taught that could be classified not as new variations, but as entirely new techniques. New forms of submission holds for the hip muscle pinch were shown by Burdikov, for the foot lock by Rudman, and for the upper arm muscle pinch by the national team wrestlers of Vilnius city during their sport camp training in 1984. Team wrestlers were independently recommended for study by the Honorable Coaches N. Novikov and V. Starshinov, who were also present to demonstrate.

Submission Hold by Pinching the Biceps

A1 One of the wrestlers is on hands and knees. The offensive wrestler is attacking from the back.

A2 The opponent catches the offensive wrestler's right leg with his right hand in the area of the Achilles tendon. The offensive wrestler uses his left hand to grab the right hand of the opponent in the area of the wrist.

A3 He then falls to his right side, keeping his grip on the hand he has grabbed.

A4 He then pushes on the muscles of the wrist and fingers of the opponent with his right leg. Applies pressure to the pinch until the opponent gives up.

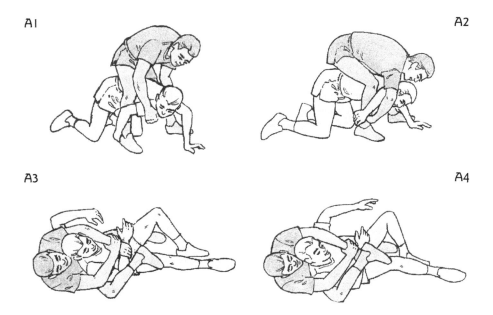

A1

A2

A3

A4

Submission Hold by Pinching the Hip Muscle

The defender is laying on his stomach. The offensive wrestler grabs the opponent's leg in the area of the cuff muscle and Achilles tendon.

B1 He then "grips" his opponent's hip by squeezing with his thighs, keeping them as close as possible to the area of the defender's buttocks.

B2-3 Then, without allowing the opponent to turn on his back, the offensive wrestler crosses his legs above his opponent's buttocks and pushes, with his own hips, the muscles of the outer and inner areas of his opponent's hips.

B4 He adds pressure to the pinch until the opponent gives up.

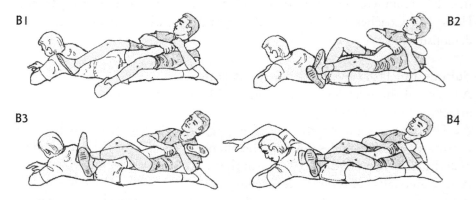

Submission Hold by Locking the Foot

C1 The opponent is leaning back supported by his hands. The offensive wrestler holds his opponent's left leg under his arm, close to his armpit.

C2 He then crosses his legs above his opponent's left leg.

C3 The offensive wrestler's arms are crossed and he leans against his opponent's ankle. The offensive wrestler arches his back and moves his left shoulder back.

C4 The pressure of the foot submission continues until the opponent feels sufficient pain to indicate submission.

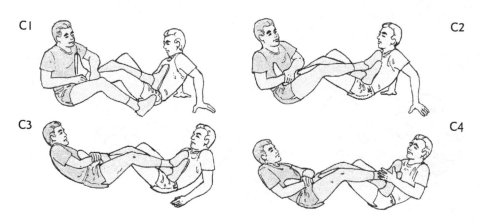

2006b). Development of sport sambo, as opposed to its paternal military version, was intended to allow practitioners to train against resistance without high risk of injury, while maintaining combat ready fitness. Since International Federation of Associated Wrestling Styles' (FILA) recognition of sambo in 1968 and the premier world sambo championships in 1973, held in Tehran, Iran, sport sambo has evolved into a nationally and internationally recognized combat sport in which military and non-military persons can participate (Scott, 2006).

Today, sambo has gained great notoriety in martial arts circles and has experienced a surge in popularity in its native Russia. This has mainly been due to the success of sambo trained mixed martial art fighters including, but not limited to the Ultimate Fighting Championships' Oleg Taktarov and Andrei Arlovski as well as Fedor Emilianenko and Sergei Kharitonov of the Pride Fighting Championships. In present day Russia promotion of sambo extends far beyond the local clubs, national training facilities, and governing bodies. Support for sambo resides deep within the Kremlin itself, where President Vladimir Putin, himself a sambo practitioner (Rudman, 2003; Putin, et al., 2004; Ignatius, 2007), has established the annual President's Cup in sambo: a national sambo tournament (I. Kurinnoy, personal communication, May 25, 2007).

In appearance, sport sambo may seem similar to modern Kodokan or Olympic judo. However, there are significant differences in rules. Similar to judo, sport sambo is a form of jacket wrestling that involves throws, pins, grappling, large joint manipulations, and submission holds. Unlike Kodokan judo, however, sport sambo disallows chokes and allows for a wide variety of leg submissions not permitted in judo (Polyakov, Yankauskas, & DeRose, 1996). Furthermore, sport sambo has far fewer gripping and time restrictions than Olympic judo and requires competitors to wear wrestling style shoes and shorts. Victory in sport sambo can come by point differential, submission hold, or Total Victory which is similar to, but more difficult to attain than judo's full point (*ippon*) due to the fact that an attacker must remain standing after completing a perfect throw. Despite these technical differences, it is common in Russia and many other countries for athletes to train sport sambo and judo simultaneously as the two sports are more similar than not.

Since first appearing at the 2000 World Sambo Championships, a competitive variant of combat sambo has developed that allows for chokes, a wider variety of submission holds, and striking within competition. This has allowed for use of many techniques that samboists often practice but which had been prohibited from use in sport sambo. Somewhat reflective of the differences between modern Olympic judo and sport sambo, many judo players have become disenchanted with continuing changes in judo's competitive rule set (Ebell, 2008) and have commented that sambo seems akin to "old school" judo (D. DeRose, personal communication, May 12, 2007).

Technical Section

One hallmark of sambo in both its sport and combat variants has been its use of rolling attacks and counter-attacks (Koepfer, 2006a). Rolling is generally considered part of any martial art training regimen if the art requires ground engagement such as falling, throwing, or grappling. Familiarity with proper rolling (and falling) is integral to a student's ability to perform and to ensure safety in any martial art that includes such variables. Oftentimes however, rolling is viewed by non-sambo practitioners as a primarily defensive tactic, an opportunity for the student to become familiar with ground movement, or even simply a method for increasing conditioning. In other words, as a matter of safety, a student must learn how to roll and move on the ground in the event that he or she is thrown, tripped, or somehow brought to the ground by an opponent (Rudman, 2003). Aside from these important goals, sambo has developed and become known for an approach to offensive rolling which promotes stealthy attacks and counter-attacks. In the following pages, I will cover the basic forward rolling technique (sometimes called shoulder roll) and three related attacks.

Forward Shoulder Roll from Kneeling Position

Forward rolling in sambo is generally taught with the notion that one may attack his or her opponent, often the opponent's legs, during or subsequent to a roll or fall. Fundamental to this concept is the notion that one stays in close range to his opponent when rolling or being thrown. Oftentimes, in non-sambo training, a forward roll is taught with the intention of rolling away from an opponent or following the energy of a given throw away from one's attacker. This is evidenced in training that involves tumbling style forward rolls in which students dive forward or over objects before completing a roll. This is certainly not incorrect and does develop strong conditioning and body/ground awareness. In fact, this type of rolling will be seen in sambo clubs as well.

However, in sambo, the notion of continuing into ground engagement immediately after being thrown or initiating a rolling attack demands that the roller not create distance between his opponent and himself, but rather minimize the distance (Koepfer, 2006a). The fact that many rolling attacks will target an opponent's legs necessitates a need for close proximity after being thrown or initiating a rolling attack. Rolling away from one's opponent will take the target leg (or other target of attack) out of reach. When rolling in this offensive manner, it should feel as if you are rolling beneath yourself and minimizing forward motion.

Ia: Start from a kneeling position.
Ib: Rolling over one shoulder, the same-side arm reaches deep between one's legs as if reaching behind one's self.
Ic: One should reach and tuck deep enough to ensure rolling "beneath one's self."
Id: Rolling out, one should prepare for a side fall position and ensure the roll is not completed

while flat on one's back.

1e: Complete the roll in a proper side fall position.

Rolling Knee Bar from a Kneeling Position

Oftentimes in sparring or competition, after a takedown or throw, one will find himself in a turtle position with the opponent attacking his exposed back. In this rolling knee bar counter-attack, the importance of rolling beneath one's self becomes evident as the target leg must be reached in order to complete the submission.

2a: Attacker (dark jacket) positions himself on the defender's back. One of the attacker's legs must be kneeling between the defender's legs to enable this rolling counter-attack.

2b: As in figures 1b-c, the defender initiates his forward roll with a deep tuck beneath himself while reaching deep between his own legs to secure the attacker's leg with his out-stretched arms (alternate view).

2c: The defender (now counter-attacking) secures and extends the attacker's leg.

2d: The defender, who has now become the attacker, finishes his roll and secures the knee bar.

Forward (Shoulder) Roll from Standing Position

Like the kneeling forward roll, the standing variation also emphasizes a deep tuck and roll beneath one's self, minimizing forward motion.

3a: Start from standing position.

3b: Starting the roll, the arm (same side as lead leg) begins to reach deep beneath one's own legs and body.

3c: As with the kneeling forward roll, one should target the shoulder of the lead arm to roll over. Importantly, the roller must tuck deeply beneath himself and reach his lead arm far behind his own legs.

3d: A deep tuck and roll will ensure that the attacker is deep enough to reach the target of the attack; which is generally behind them as in the rolling knee bar cited earlier. This depth of roll also ensures that the roll will sufficiently penetrate beneath the target's hips and unbalance him or her.

3e: Like the kneeling forward roll, one should come out of the roll on one's side, not flat one's back.

3f: Complete the roll in a proper side fall position.

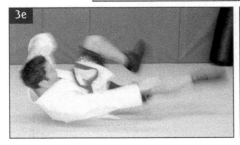

Rolling Arm Bar Attack on Turtle Position

In this technique, the need to roll deep beneath one's self from a standing position is clearly apparent.

4a: The attacker (white) begins in a cross-body position on the opponent's rounded back with a grip on the back of his opponent's collar.

4b: The attacker steps over his opponent (with the leg nearest to his opponent's hips) and secures a grip on his belt. The attacker's leg should now be between his arms.

4c: The attacker must now, in a sudden motion, lift his opponent off the mat in order to create space and position his leg beneath his opponent and prepare for a forward roll.

4d: As in figures 3c & 3d, the attacker must tuck his leg and forward roll deeply beneath himself and his opponent. It is important that the attacker's roll come immediately after his lift and there is no gap in timing for the opponent to counter the attack. Equally important is that the attacker does not lose his belt and collar grips as they, along with his tucked leg, will force his opponent to roll with him.

4e: Coming out of the roll, the attacker releases his collar grip so he may pass his free leg over his opponent's face and secure the arm bar.

4f: Finishing the roll, the attacker must squeeze his knees tightly to secure the arm, hug the arm tightly to his body, and extend his hips to complete the arm bar.

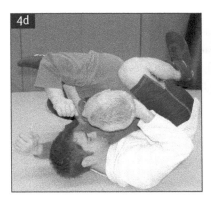

Rolling Podvhat or Kick-up Throw

In this throw, which is very similar to judo's *uchimata*, one can see the importance of a committed forward rolling motion and deep tuck.

5a: From the clinch, the attacker (dark jacket) secures over-the-back and sleeve grips on his opponent. The attacker should use the over-the-back grip to load his opponent by dropping his weight.

5b: Entering for the throw, the attacker's leg (same side as the back gripping arm) must penetrate deeply between his opponent's legs, while pulling his opponent's arm forward and across his torso. The over-the-back grip will make this a very tight clinch, but the attacker's hips must also penetrate towards and beneath the defender's hips. In combination with the load of the over-the-back grip, the attacker's forward pull of the arm and backward penetration of the leg/hips offers the proper circular energy needed to unbalance the opponent.

5c: In this figure, we see how deep the attacker must lean/roll into the throw. Unlike other types of kick-up throws, the over-the-back grip will tightly secure the defender and allow for the combination of forward rolling motion, use of gravity, and kick-up of the penetrating leg to bring the defender into the throw.

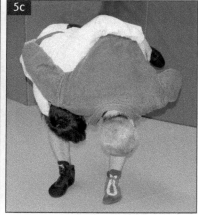

5d: The attacker continues rolling/throwing his opponent, as both men become airborne. Also evident is how the attacker's over-the-back gripping arm is reminiscent of the tucking arm in the standing forward roll (see figure 3c). Like the standing forward roll, in this throw, the shoulder of the over-the-back gripping arm becomes the target shoulder in the forward roll/throwing motion.

5e: Coming out of the throw/roll, the attacker must be sure to release the over-the-back grip and secure a stable top position on his opponent. This will generally be a modified side fall position.

5f: From here, the attacker can then determine which top position is best and most appropriate at the time of roll out.

5g: In this case, the attacker transitions to a cross-body position.

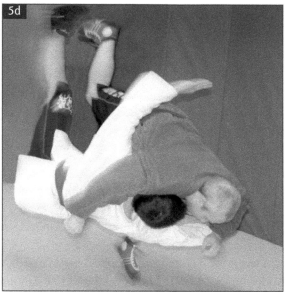

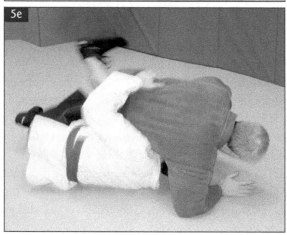

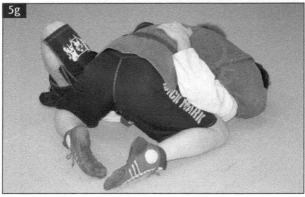

References

Ebell, S. B. (2008). Competition versus tradition in kodokan judo. *Journal of Asian Martial Arts*, *17*(1), 28-37.

Ignatius, A. (2007, December 31). A tsar is born. *Time*, *170* (27), 46-62.

Jacques, B. and Anderson, S. (1999). The development of sambo in Europe and America. *Journal of Asian Martial Arts*, 8(2), 20-41.

Koepfer, S. (2006a, April). Classic sambo. *Ultimate Grappling*, 6(4), 66-67.

Koepfer, S. (2006b, April). Struggling to survive: Can FILA end sambo's civil war? *Ultimate Grappling*, 6(4), 76-80, 127.

Polyakov, L., Yankauskas, I., and DeRose, D. (1996). The variety of submission holds developed and applied by leading sambo practitioners. *Journal of Asian Martial Arts*, 5(3), 52-57.

Putin, V., Shestakov, V., Levitsky, A., and Russell, G. (2004). *Judo: History, theory, practice*. Berkeley, CA: North Atlantic Books.

Rudman, D. (2003). *Sambo (self defense without weapons): From Viktor Spiridonov to Vladimir Putin* (V. Kulikov & I. Kulikov, Trans.). Moscow: n.p. Out of print.

Scott, S. (2006). *Championship sambo: Submission holds and ground fighting*. Hartford: Turtle Press.

index